W9-AAI-887

THE SEVEN AXIOMS OF VALUE CREATION

IAN KHAN

ISBN-13: 9781987411478

#change

the only permanent thing in the universe

For my wife Sabeen, who helps me to be who I am.

Disclaimer

This is a work of fiction. Names, characters, businesses, places, events, and incidents are either the products of the author's imagination or used in a fictitious manner. Any resemblance to actual persons, living or dead, or actual events is purely coincidental.

CONTENTS

INTRODUCTION

We are at the cusp of the fourth Industrial Revolution, a time when man and machine will truly collaborate to create outcomes never seen before. Technologies such as the Internet of Things, Artificial Intelligence, Cloud, Blockchain, and others will combine to form a world that we can imagine somewhat yet do not completely comprehend. As a race, we humans are also responsible for changing the state of affairs at a global level, as global problems are now affecting us locally. Pollution, nuclear radiation, climate change, hunger, poverty, refugee crises, war—these affect us all, no matter where they originated. Hence, to change where we live and how we live, we cannot ignore the rest of the world.

Today more than ever we need to come together and rewrite the basic rules of the game. We need to act differently to make a different tomorrow, because wishing for a new future while we fail to change our actions is nothing but foolish.

Organizations and individuals collectively have to partner together in re-creating the foundation on which the idea of modern work is based, to be successful in the true sense—to be value creators.

PART 1

1

WE HAVE ARRIVED:
SWEET BELLS OF HEAVEN

Ding, ding, ding, ding! The opening bell at
NASDAQ this June 14th was one of the best
sounds Max had ever heard. The last few years had
been grueling, and all the hard work had finally
paid off. The endless pitches to venture capital
firms, investor meetings, shareholder briefings, and
countless advisory meetings had finally culminated
in the submission of an initial public offering (IPO)
by Rickshaw, Inc.

As the opening bell rang out on the NASDAQ
stage that morning, Max couldn't help but think
of his mother, who had stood by him all these years
and helped him become the man he now was. He
was eternally grateful for all she had done for him.
But she had passed away six months ago after a

long battle with cancer. Max looked up, teary eyed, and felt certain she was watching over him.

At his side, his wife squeezed his hand. When he looked at her, he saw teary eyes, a reflection of his own. They had made it and she could not have been more proud of him. Like any couple, Max and Aira had endured struggles in their twelve years of marriage, but they had emerged a strong team who supported each other.

Aira had been instrumental in helping Max launch Rickshaw, a company that understood value creation in today's digital times. Max and his team had worked relentlessly to create a platform that provided more than just products and technologies, but changed the way technology was consumed by end users. His team had pushed the grain to lead the market with a blue ocean strategy that Max was passionate about. They had finally hit pay dirt, and the biggest validation of their success came today as they released an oversubscribed IPO on the stock exchange.

But the journey Max was celebrating today went back much further than the launch of Rickshaw. You could say, it went back a hundred years, when one man and his entire family left behind everyone they knew to trek over the Muztagh Mountains in search of a better life.

That man was named Asraf Pasha, and he was Max's great-grandfather. Asraf belonged to the Khan tribe from the northwestern region of the Karakoram mountain range spanning the borders of Pakistan, India, and China. He had heard of a lush valley in Kashmir that was Heaven on earth. Fertile lands, lakes full of fresh, clean water, and an abundance of lush vegetation… this was a place where he and his family could live a happy life. To get there, though, he would have to lead his family over four mountain passes in one of the most treacherous terrains in the world.

The journey was long and arduous, day after day of walking in high altitude and low temperatures. But Asraf was fixed on his goal, and step by step, they finally reached that beautiful valley.

Decades later, Max was born there. His was a happy childhood. His father, Aslam, was a well-respected civil engineer who did very well through government contracts, and he ensured Max and his brothers were educated at the best schools, to equip them for success.

But little had Asraf known when he crossed the mountains to Kashmir that this land was suffering under a ruthless king who cared little for his subjects. Finally, Aslam decided it was time to follow his grandfather's example and take his family to a better place: the land of opportunity.

Twenty years after setting foot on American soil as an immigrant, Max was ringing the bell at NASDAQ, a landmark achievement for any entrepreneur. And it was not luck that brought him there; his success belonged to him entirely.

2

COMMITTING TO LIFELONG LEARNING IS MANDATORY

As the echo of the NASDAQ bell began to wane, Max looked at the few hundred people on the stock exchange floor, ready to work through the intricacies of one of the world's most prominent financial platforms. He remembered what Mr. Green, his high school teacher and one of his early mentors, always said to him:

"Success will not come to you one fine day and say, 'Here I am.' There is no such thing as luck; that's just what unsuccessful people call it when hardworking people finally reach their goal. Their so-called 'luck' is the intersection of preparation and opportunity. You have to prepare for success, for that opportunity of a lifetime, so that when the opportunity for success knocks at your door, you're ready."

Mr. Green could not have been more correct. Max had worked relentlessly over the past decade or so to build what had culminated in a company listed on NASDAQ. He was successful today because he had prepared for success—he had worked for it.

When we see successful people, we often have one of three reactions: we feel angry with regret because we don't have what we want; we envy their success, yet feel happy for them; or we get inspired by their success and want to follow in their footsteps. Success, as Max realized, is not a get-rich-quick scheme; it is not something that happens overnight, or without careful planning. Success in any aspect of life—personal or business—is the outcome of a carefully calibrated balance of both excellence and expertise in something that you are passionate about and have honed specific skills for. It will probably take you weeks, months, or even years to reach your optimum level of expertise, and it will potentially be second nature to you to excel in the endeavors in which you want to succeed.

Take the example of any profession—and there are many to choose from. How about a pediatric neurosurgeon?

A pediatric neurosurgeon, very simply put, becomes a doctor first of all. For at least five to seven years, they study medicine to earn a first degree, and then they can treat people who were sick and create value in their lives by providing them with constructive advice regarding any health concern.

The doctor then specializes in neurosurgery, which makes them an expert in diagnosing brain conditions and operating on brains. This learning takes a few years to master, if you are committed enough and have sufficient interest in neurosurgery in the first place. No amount of outside motivation or persuasion could push anyone to be a neurosurgeon if they weren't committed. You have got to really want to be a neurosurgeon.

Finally, the already skilled neurosurgeon specializes further in a very specific niche in healthcare: treating the brain-related conditions of children. This takes more years of intense work within neurosurgery, together with researching and learning everything specific to children and their brains.

At the end of many years of preparation and skill-building, the neurosurgeon reaches a stage where their probability of success in treating a two-year-old child with a brain defect is the highest in the world compared to any other surgeon. The pediatric neurosurgeon in this case has perfected their skill.

Like the pediatric neurosurgeon, you have to prepare yourself and hone your expertise to reach a stage where every single cell in your body is ready for that next opportunity or challenge when it knocks on your door. This is the best possible way to succeed. In fact, it is the *only* way to succeed. Pave the path to your success by mastering your craft, giving it everything you have and raising your competency to a level where you feel ready to tackle any challenge in that area of expertise.

Apply this thinking to your life and ask yourself: *What do I need in order to become an expert?* You could be a hair stylist, a businessperson, a painter, a baker, an engineer, a salesperson, or a librarian. You could be in a position where you are performing a general task that many other people are doing, such as working as a cashier in a grocery store or selling tickets at a museum kiosk; or you could be working in a highly specialized area that only a handful of people would even understand. Whatever your circumstances, this is the universal truth: You will only be successful in your career if you commit to learning the art of your trade at the highest level possible, and you continue to tirelessly build your knowledge and skills to be better every day. You may or may not become one of the only people who knows the skill, but one thing is guaranteed: You will massively increase the probability of your success with every opportunity that knocks on your door in the future.

3

NEW THINGS ARE SOMETIMES NOT ENTIRELY NEW

Two years had passed since Max had listed his company on NASDAQ, and Rickshaw had grown into a sizeable organization. Fourteen thousand employees in six countries and revenues of over five billion and government contracts was a great achievement for Max. They had 'turned into a unicorn' in less than three years.

In addition, Max was working with large philanthropic organizations doing work in some of the neediest regions of the world. He was inspired by other philanthropists of the world who had committed millions to causes such as eradicating malaria in Africa. For Max, the need to give back was more crucial than anything else. The nature of charities, as he saw it, was that you needed to be accountable for every dollar, and unless you saw that dollar as a smile or clothing on someone, it had no validation.

With a zeal to give back, Max had made a personal commitment to charities working in the Kashmir region in particular. The Kashmir region had seen some heavy devastation in recent years—infrastructure, schools, even entire villages destroyed. Yet after the Western war on Al-Qaeda and Isis, it had been left to fend for itself. These were Max's people, and he felt a responsibility to help.

Max was supporting the construction of infrastructure for educational institutions in the remote high-altitude areas of the region. The biggest ambition was to construct a regional school that would serve over 2,000 students and provide vocational hands-on training in technology, which would get the students ready to tackle the outside world and find opportunities.

Meanwhile, back in America, Max was working very closely with some health foundations that cared for challenged kids. He had also invested in a few startups through an incubator, focusing on healthcare-related apps that would leverage the power of the internet with products to service the healthcare industry.

At 3:00 one morning, Max was woken by the phone ringing.

"Hello?" he answered.

"Max, it's John... from Health Ventures. I need your help. We have fifteen tons of supplies held up at the border in Cambodia. They won't let them pass. These are for the refugees, and we've been working very hard to put them together, but now we seem to have hit a brick wall. I hate to bother you, but it looks like we've run out of options."

This John Gardener, an old friend of Max's from university. A brilliant man with a great drive to help underprivileged communities all over the world. John had been involved in causes from the beginning of his adulthood, when he became a member of Greenpeace. He'd pulled all kinds of stunts to get the attention he needed, from sticking a large hammer on a ship to sailing through the Arctic. His work had now taken him to Asia, where he was working with communities to solve the refugee crisis from Burma. The Rohingya had long been a target community, and after years of persecution they were steadily overflowing into neighboring countries, including Thailand and Cambodia, where John was active.

"No worries, John," said Max. "Do you have perishables in the supplies?"

"Yes," replied John. "We have over five tons of food items that may go bad within a week."

"I'm on it," said Max, as he quickly scanned his mind for the best people to contact. He remembered an old friend who worked as the special attaché at the Canadian embassy in Phuket, and told John the man's name.

"When you call, tell him I referred you. He may be your man. In the meantime, I'll do what I can from here," said Max, his mind still whirring.

"I can't thank you enough for this, Max. I'll speak to you later, my friend," John said.

"It's my pleasure," said Max, and he hung up the phone.

After that call, Max couldn't get back to sleep. He kept thinking about the state of this world where food, shelter, and essentials were completely inaccessible to many. *We should be able to do better as a race,* he thought. *We've come a long way from the time of the Neanderthals, so why is there still such an imbalance?* He argued with himself and wrestled with the issues until dawn.

Max spent the rest of that day contemplating the state of his project and the fact that he could be doing so much more, given his position and influence as a technology leader. He believed that problems always have a solution, and that there are always opportunities to change the status quo. With that in mind, he had created the motto of his organization: "Let's change someone's world today."

The idea of being capable is important when it comes to creating change. The ability to realize we are capable of doing something has a lot to do with what we have been exposed to.

Take, for example, a research scientist who works hard to find the cure for a disease. They may never know they have found the cure unless their discovery is reinforced by the various mechanisms required to support it. During the time and phase of undergoing this process, they need access to labs, crucial knowledge, other research, a way to accelerate results, and, finally, to conduct pilot tests or clinical trials, before mass commercial production. This whole chain of events is oversimplified, but the idea is to illustrate that one simple idea needs a host of supporting mechanisms for it to succeed in a substantial way. Massive success is achieved only by doing things that matter with the right approach.

At the core of the research someone does is the question, 'why?' What is driving them to do this research and how do they intend to change the world? What drives the researcher to stay in their lab for tens of hours at a stretch, going through thousands of steps, processes, and procedures hundreds of times, until they actually have some sort of breakthrough?

The answer to 'why?' lies in discovering your true passion and aligning yourself with a greater cause at a personal level. People always have a lot of drive when they align themselves with the best base goal for them. This philosophy can be driven by each of the seven key areas at the core of the meaningful conversation system.

4

THE MOST IMPORTANT THINGS IN LIFE MAY ACTUALLY BE SIMPLE

If you have ever thought that your life could be simpler and were really disappointed by the complexity of things around you, there is good news. Life actually is much simpler than we sometimes make it. Unless we realize that, though, we will never have the pleasure of enjoying simple yet powerful things.

Here are some basic axioms that we can take as they are, without fighting them and without overanalyzing them:

1. Kindness is the key to being satisfied.

2. Self-actualization is simple.

3. Knowledge is powerful.

4. Family is everything.

5. The earth is our home.

6. Be valuable to others.

7. Be grateful no matter what.

These key tenets were the basis of Max's life philosophy.

How do you align yourself with any of these seven core areas? Do you feel strongly about any one of them? Have you been influenced by someone or some event that drives you more towards a specific area?

It is also possible that you do not align well with any of the axioms. Perhaps you feel they are not relevant to you and your life. Many of you may say:

"I am not affected by any of these things, because they are just not part of who I am. I know there are people suffering somewhere in the world, but I cannot be responsible for everyone. So leave me be and let me take care of my family."

Some people feel they don't have enough time to think about these things, because they are far too busy managing kids, work, marriage, social lives, and more. Others may have other reasons.

If you don't connect to even a single one of these axioms, it is because your personal life philosophy does not align to any of these ideas. Should your philosophy align? Let's find out...

5

THE NEED FOR DEVELOPING A PERSONAL LIFE PHILOSOPHY

A personal life philosophy is what drives your life when you are doing nothing. This is the automatic programing—like a guiding mechanism—that helps you go in the right direction, even when you let go of the controls. Imagine this being a giant but non-aggressive magnet of life that will always draw you to it, no matter which direction you are going. It is the gentle pull that keeps you in a certain frame of mind.

Believe it or not, we all have a life philosophy that drives us. If yours does not align with any of the seven guiding principles, don't worry. Most likely it does, but you have not realized it yet. We need to discover more about you first.

Becoming aware of your personal life philosophy may dramatically change you as a person, as you come to fully understand who you are and why you do the things you do. Your life philosophy governs both what you do and how you go about it.

Let's do a simple exercise to find out what you do align with. First, find a quiet and comfortable place. To get in the zone, close your eyes and take a few deep breaths, exhaling slowly. Then take a blank piece of paper and draw a table with two columns. In the first column, write down each of the seven axioms from above.

Here is the exercise:

1. Think about your life and how it is right now. Visualize your family, your friends, all your relationships. Try to think about an average day that you spend with your colleagues, friends, and family. Think of how you feel.

2. Take the first axiom and superimpose it on your vision of your life. For example, imagine you become one of the many people who suffer in the world. You are on the streets, homeless, without any shelter or clean, dry clothes. Imagine your day. Think of your family and how they would feel. Think about the quality of your life. Let your imagination run wild.

3. Using a scale of 0 to 10, with 10 being the most uncomfortable feeling, note down

in the second column how uncomfortable Step 2 made you feel.

4. Repeat Steps 2 and 3 for the other six axioms.

Hopefully, you had a good session imagining the seven core tenets. How did you do? Which topic got the most points? Why? Do you realize that you just stumbled upon your core beliefs at a very superficial level and found out some of the things that really bother you? These are also things you do not want for yourself.

This is the zone where personal life philosophy starts taking shape. You can do this exercise as deeply as you like and as many times as you want. The more frequently you do the exercise, and the more deeply you consider the issues and your feelings, the better able you are to fine-tune your own knowledge about yourself, which is precisely the goal.

There are many other techniques that allow you to go deeper into your mind. Meditation, prayer, yoga, exercise, and long walks in nature are a few examples. You can use any technique you like, and most likely you will get the same results with each of them.

6

BUILDING YOUR OWN PERSONAL LIFE PHILOSOPHY

Imagine that you are building the ship of your dreams in order to go on a long journey of adventure off into the unknown that will take years, maybe even a lifetime. On your voyage you will encounter new cultures and people, and beauty, as well as things that challenge and sadden you, like poverty and war.

Now, while building this ship you work with the best architects and shipbuilders. They give you the best possible advice on how to make this ship and what you need on board in order to succeed on your journey. The rudder of this ship is your personal life philosophy. It is the part that will guide this colossal ship to its destination. The rudder is key to going anywhere and doing anything. It's the only thing that will send your ship in the right direction.

Be it a stormy or sunny day, the rudder will keep your ship on track towards any destination that you plan to reach.

Often the simplest things are tremendously powerful, and so it is with the personal life philosophy. In essence, we all have this philosophy, whether we know it or not, and we use it to make every decision in our lives. Our core philosophy has brought us to where we are, and it continues to power our thoughts and actions at the most profound level.

Start building your philosophy if you have not already. Now is the time. Age, financial condition, family status—none of these determine whether you should build your philosophy. If you are human, you absolutely need to lock this down, right now.

7

BE READY FOR WHEN OPPORTUNITY KNOCKS

Max had been invited to speak at a conference in a small Swiss town. Not just any conference: It would bring together some of the greatest thinkers and influencers, to discuss how the world should change. This would be a masterclass for Max in the personal life philosophies of great men and women, a chance to share ideas with them and learn from them.

While Max was excited, he was tense about the extent of this opportunity and how he would speak about what drove him mad with obsession. There were far too many important things to talk about, and to refine them into a speech that would resonate was a tough task. Nevertheless, this was the opportunity of a lifetime and Max felt extremely privileged to have been invited to speak.

Just a month from now, he would be in front of a global audience, sharing his ideas about which technologies would propel the future. At his heart, Max was a humanist more than anything, and even though his mark on technology was profound, his core beliefs were always about empowering people and realizing their true potential, himself included. As a child, Max had learned from his father to give 100 percent, to always do his best, whatever the circumstances. He would do his best at the conference, just as he had done his best to earn a place at that conference.

Because in fact Max's journey to this conference had started a few years ago. He had been prepared for opportunity to knock—identifying the opportunity, and then going after it. Yes, it had taken him a while to get where he was, but with the right combination of effort, follow-up, and a subsequent favorable series of incidents, he had managed to connect with the right people and share his ideas. He remembered that success has nothing to do with luck, but everything to do with preparation. It was this preparation that got him the opportunity to speak at the conference.

8

WHAT IS BETTER THAN ASKING THE UNIVERSE TO PROVIDE?

People often think that success comes easily to others, while they stagnate and are deprived of the good things in life. Be it more money, cars, wealth in general, or other things, some people have it all while others don't. If that is your mindset then you absolutely need to change it, because it is not the truth.

Many years ago, a popular book and subsequent documentary took over the world stage, creating waves about being able to achieve anything you want by simply asking the universe for it. Top gurus and pundits spoke in that documentary about how you could create this reality and make things appear in your life simply by being positive. We wish it were this simple and true.

The idea of the universe being able to provide is a great theory, but it is not explained 100 percent. To understand this, you really need to consider a quotation from Carl Sagan. (If you don't know who Carl was, well, let's just say that he was one of the greatest visionaries and futurists the world has seen in modern times. His insights into cosmology and astronomy were greater than anything we had ever seen, and he made these known through a series of books and novels he wrote. Put simply, Carl Sagan is a legend.) Carl said: "We are made from star-stuff." So, we are made from the same material that the stars and planets are made from. Our bodies are part of the vast universe, which essentially is all around us, and being made from the same material makes us a key part of it.

There are many theories, such as the double-slit experiment, that consider the relationship between matter and parallel universes, and how the power of thought can change the way things behave. This is a complex discussion and not necessarily the object of this book. But going back to the question of the universe being able to provide us with everything we need, the two ideas need to be combined: first, that we are part of the universe, and second, that as the observers of things around us, we can change their very nature.

Now, we started with the idea of being able to achieve anything we want, and how the universe would help us to get it. We have also understood that there are no chance encounters, no lucky scenarios, but planned episodes of events that get realized when the right things align. Imagine that you are a really great sword maker, the best in the whole country. It would not be a surprise if tomorrow you got the opportunity to make a sword for one of the greatest warriors of all time, because he happened to pass through your town, discovered that you were right there, and realized that he had the opportunity to work with you and get a sword made. In this case, we could say that you got lucky because you made a sword for the world's greatest warrior, but we could also say that you honed your skills over a lifetime and then one day the right opportunity presented itself to you. It is a matter of perception.

If you look at successful people in the world, you will find a common thread of success between them. This common thread is that they have worked very hard for a very long time to prove who they are and to be the best in their field. Richard Branson, Bill Gates, Warren Buffet, and even Taylor Swift are all people who have worked very hard to get where they are. Now, being the best at something has a lot of advantages. You get access to a lot more opportunities, and when opportunity knocks, guess who is ready with their skills? It is a cycle and a mindset.

9

DRAGON-SLAYERS AND OLD LADIES

Let's agree to change our mindset in order to believe that success can be achieved with careful planning and honing of our skills. We also need to interact with the world outside and find opportunities to do the *other* thing needed in this golden mix. Any idea what that is?

Let me ask you: What do a knight slaying the evil dragon who terrorized a village and a neighbor helping a little old lady with her groceries have in common? Looking at the big picture, you see that one person is doing something that is benefiting the other (or others).

The dragon is a constant threat, eating people, destroying homes, and setting things on fire. It is terrorizing the village and creating constant havoc. The one thing the villagers need more than anything else is for this dragon to be gone. The hero knight steps in and slays the dragon. He 'creates value.'

What about the old grandma? Well, for Granny, things like going to the market have become difficult. What she needs during this time of failing health is for someone to help her with such tasks. By helping her, the neighbor 'creates value.'

Value creation is the subject of much research and many a thesis around the globe. It makes for a popular topic because everyone wants to know how to be the best in order to create positive change. Just in case you are curious, here is a definition of value creation by economist Georgescu-Roegen:

A pattern of matter, energy, and/or information has economic value if the following three conditions are jointly met:

1. **Irreversibility:** *All value-creating economic transformations and transactions are thermodynamically irreversible.*

2. **Entropy:** *All value-creating economic transformations and transactions reduce entropy locally within the economic system, while increasing entropy globally.*

3. **Fitness:** *All value-creating economic transformations and transactions produce artifacts and/or actions that are fit for human purpose.*

Simply stated, value is created when we change the nature of things and help to create a positive change through an action. This change can be temporary or permanent, but it must have changed the status quo. That's all we need to remember.

In business, value creation is closely tied to economic and financial benefit. As such, any activity that ultimately changes the financial elements of the equation is a value creation change. Now, if you think about this for a moment, you will realize that every business is driven by dollars, and the ultimate goal of every business is to be able to change this financial equation. This is done by generating revenue through the various ways in which the business operates. The business could use the older brick-and-mortar method or new e-commerce-based ideas; either way, the goal is the same: generate revenue, linking value creation closely to the economical side of the business. Take a moment and think about any profession that comes to mind. It provides a product or service to its customers and ultimately exchanges money. The value is driven in two ways: On the customer's side, their core situation changes as a result of this transaction, and on the business's side, revenue is generated.

Our goal here is not to lay down a PhD thesis on value creation, but to understand the basics so that we think about how the digital era has changed the journey and what that means for us.

10

LEARN HOW TO RECOGNIZE OPPORTUNITIES

"They want me to talk about value creation," said Max to Aira as they sat on the porch after dinner. "I know how to define it, but it's a complex topic. I'm not certain they would understand what I mean. I've so wanted to speak at the conference, and now it's happening. Maybe I need to rethink how to do this. I will talk to Cynthia; maybe she can help."

Cynthia was a speech coach Max had utilized to iron out some rough spots in his talk to employees when they hit their first billion dollars in revenue. Those were exciting times.

"I think you need to look deeper," said Aira. "You know what this is all about. I know you think you need help, but it's all there inside. Why don't you take some time off instead?"

"That's a great idea. I need to visit Kashmir and see how things are going with the orphanage."

"Sounds good," said Aira, and she retired for the night.

Max left his mind drift as he looked up at the stars above, like a giant carpet of twinkling dots. He loved spending time by himself, because it gave him time to reflect on his life and think about what he wanted to do, and he loved to be close to nature. Max often went on treks in the hills around the city, and he had also hiked extensively in the Andes and the Alps with Aira. Being born and raised in the midst of the Himalayas, Max was naturally in tune with nature.

His current plan was to give back to his birthplace by constructing a series of orphanages. The war over the last two decades had created a huge need to accommodate children whose parents died as a result of the conflict. Max knew a trip to Kashmir was long overdue.

Two months later, Max was preparing to fly to Kashmir. He had lined up a series of meetings with key people on the ground who would help him get the orphanage up and running. This was a good cause that would bring positive change to the children and to their communities. Max was passionate about the project and really helping the place he had grown up, where he still felt a strong sense of belonging.

During the trip, he was also planning to spend some time in his favorite place in the world, Pahalgam. He wanted some time alone, to reconsider his life and how he could best make a difference and create value.

11

IDENTIFY WHAT BRINGS YOU TRUE JOY

For many of us, passionately pursuing a dream is a difficult task. We are hindered by negative emotions and self-sabotage. Creating value requires aligning yourself with a basic value system with which you identify. This, in turn, is based on your core beliefs, the majority of which are created during childhood. Have you ever wondered how some people so passionately pursue a dream? Despite the task being difficult, they are able to go far with apparent ease and get results. The answer lies not in how easy the path is or how lucky they get, but in one simple thing: Their goal aligns with their core beliefs, it relates to what they hold dear in their heart.

The question is, do you know how to tap into your core beliefs and core value system?

When NASA launches a space shuttle, it needs to know the purpose of this mission. The simple answer? To launch a space shuttle that will go to the International Space Station, deliver supplies, collect data, and then return. Simple. Next, NASA takes maybe a year or two to put the entire plan into action and essentially make this come true. Everyone who works on this project is aligned to this one single goal. Everyone's activities are aligned to this single thing that needs to be done— launching the space shuttle. That's how NASA succeeds. That's how every high-functioning organization succeeds: by aligning people's tasks with the main goal.

Many times, though, aligning is more difficult than this. People are not machines and they cannot quickly be reconfigured to align. They have different value and belief systems that need to be accessed, in order to get the best out of them. In the case of organizations, unless you tap into the potential of people and find alignment between the organization's mission and the value system of your people, things will not work out. Now you may ask, how does an organization tap into the value systems of hundreds of employees and create a single mission that aligns to all of them? The answer is simple: You don't. Instead, you build your organization on the core tenets of everyone. This is how value creation works.

Organizations today spend billions of dollars on ensuring their corporate culture resonates with their employees, and rightfully so. Employees are the fuel that drive the organization to execute its mission and they pass on the value the organization seeks to create as a result of what it offers. There is a distinct chain of command that passes from the top down, from leaders to executors at the ground level. This is the 10,000-foot view of the chain of value creation. We are not specifically talking about revenue generation here—although for organizations, money is an essential part of how they see value being generated for them—but looking at a different side of value creation.

12

TIME TO BE HONEST

Ultimately, what contributes to any kind of value creation is the human element. We, as people, contribute to any given circumstance and impact the situation to deliver value. The responsibilities and roles of people have been shifting as different areas of value creation open up.

A few thousand years ago, we did things in a different way, and our priorities and thoughts were completely different. There was no automation in industry, and everything we did was manual and labor intensive. Despite this, we achieved a lot of things, including great feats—such as building the Pyramids, which definitely served a purpose when they were built. Technology developments in the last two decades have changed things in a way never seen before. We now have automation to the level where the microprocessors that help to power all the devices we use in our everyday lives are being manufactured by the millions every single day. What about some of the even more basic things, such as electricity, cars, airplanes, and buildings? These are innovations and devices as well, and they all serve a purpose. None of these were available a few hundred years ago, and most are the direct result of technology, automation, and innovation as part of the various industrial revolutions. These things and many others have resulted from a change in the idea of value creation. The way we make things happen today is very different from how we did things in the past.

Look back just a few decades and take a few minutes to think about some of the things that were different then. There were no computers, cellphones, flat-screen TVs, Netflix, smartphones, ticket-booking websites, online shopping, eBay, Amazon, smart cars, internet banking, and a million other things. Life was simple, black and white, and manual. It is amazing how much progress has occurred in such a short amount of time.

This progress has happened as a result of a massive amount of work people put in, in different places around the world, in different ways, and through different ideas and initiatives. Some things were invented in the heart of America, while others were invented in India. Some things first saw the light of day in China, others in Japan. Collectively, we as a human race were able to create a massive push to make the new technological revolution a possibility. How did we end up doing this in so many places at the same time? How did we think of doing this all together? It is all because of the power of collaboration and thought-sharing. People from different places collaborated on their ideas. They worked on problems globally, transmitting ideas across the oceans through the mail and phone calls, and meeting personally. This took a lot of work and it is still happening right now, but with mediums such as the internet, there is now a much faster speed of execution.

We also found a way to align our life values and goals to the causes that we liked. For example, someone who was inclined to help eradicate disease found new organizations to work with that had initiatives supporting this cause. People who were passionate about transportation found a way to work with car manufacturers and create the new generation of cars we see on the roads today. This happened millions of times around the world, involving millions of people. This is how the world changed a little bit every second, to get to where it is right now. This may seem obvious, but it is worth revisiting in order to see the full context.

People will always be human. What I mean by this is that we will always think from a human perspective. (We hear a lot today about automation and machines, and how artificial intelligence will take over our work. Should we be afraid? What do you think? I will give you my perspective on this later in the book.) So, being people, we will always be driven by ideas, values, and thoughts. Remember that rudder from the ship of dreams? It is this rudder that will define what you do and which direction you take.

There are two ways in which organizations can tap into human potential and create value for others. The first is to work on things that people relate to, that people are already aligned with. An example of this may be an organization working on eradicating poverty or educating communities. They then have to create a cause-related business around the idea. The second way is to create a cause, create something new—invent a new thought or base belief system. This is harder to do; in fact, it may not be possible at all, because every value we would ever need has already been created. Give it some thought.

For both organizations as well as individuals, this convergence of thought into a single idea or towards a single case is a fundamental reason for connecting.

13

YOU CAN CREATE AMAZING THINGS

When two or more entities come together as a result of their values aligning, true magic happens. This is true for people, causes, organizations, and anything else you may think of that needs to come together. This is not a case of black and white, or yin and yang, but a simple convergence of ideas.

Now, during an average day, how many times do you ask yourself: *Does this align with my values?* Consciously, probably not many times; but subconsciously, perhaps thousands of times. Your subconscious mind has an innate capability to make decisions for you and influence anything that you do in your day. The human mind is one of the most complex things in the world, far greater in complexity than all the computers put together.

The amount of automated decision-making that occurs is mind-boggling.

On top of that, add all the learning you have done throughout your life, from way back in childhood to now. Remember your mom's pumpkin pie? The taste still lingers in some corner of your brain, as do all the heartbreaks and other memories you have. These memories are part of the overall life experiences you've had—and the natural result is who you are. If you took away all of your thoughts, memories, and experiences, you would be left as only a body with no identity.

Going back to values, anything and everything that has happened to you is part of your value system. How you lived as a child and what your parents taught you laid the foundations for your value system, but more recent experiences count too. For example, say you had a terrible experience five years ago, and that experience created a strong dislike for an activity, so you do not enjoy it at all anymore. Not all values are formed in childhood, but many are, and more build up as we go along.

Your value system is key in shaping your destiny... just like Max.

Max stood on the tarmac ready to board his plane. He flew mostly business class these days, but was not a huge fan of flying at all, feeling it was largely a waste of money. Despite having amassed a fortune,

Max was still humble at heart. The flight boarded and Max was all set to travel to Kashmir, a place he had cherished throughout his life, and one that had shaped his character in a number of ways.

After a long flight, Max would have a quick stopover in Brussels, before he was to board a plane for the second leg of his trip. This plane was a private one. A generous friend, Silas Arnato, head of securities at a large European bank, had offered to pick him up while he flew from Amsterdam to New Delhi. Max could not refuse, as their friendship went back a long way, to when Silas was based in San Francisco and worked in a venture firm. They had formed a close bond when Max initially started his company, and Silas helped raise funds, essentially handling all aspects of the finances. Although they lived far from each other now, they still managed to meet every now and then. They were close friends.

It was three p.m. as the plane touched down. Max woke to an air stewardess's voice crackling though the PA system as she welcomed everyone to Brussels. He could hear some passengers already clicking away at their seat belts, even though the plane was still moving on the taxiway. Max could never understand why people always lined up to disembark an aircraft long before it had come to a stop. *We'll all get off soon enough. What's the rush?* he would think.

Max was halfway through his journey and had even managed to get a little shuteye on the flight. He was excited now as he thought about his destination and what was bringing him there. He had spent most of the flight reminiscing over his childhood and the state of Kashmir just before his family left. Many years had passed, but his memories were still fresh.

Two hours later, Max was on board *The Kristoff*, a Gulfstream G280 aircraft, which was small yet powerful enough to fly at Mach 0.85 and had an impressive range of 6,667 kilometers. They would just make it to New Delhi without any need to refuel.

"Good morning, sir," the captain greeted Max in his stiff British accent. "Welcome aboard *The Kristoff*. Mr. Arnato sends his apologies. His plans changed at the last minute and he couldn't come. He said you would understand."

"Oh, I hope everything's alright," said Max.

"Yes, of course, sir. Just a work-related matter of some urgency he had to attend to. I hope we can continue our journey and take you to your destination, sir," said the captain.

"Yes, Captain, and thank you," said Max.

They took off shortly after, and Max found himself thinking of a vacation he and Aira had shared a few years ago in Morocco. It had been a great time, as they had enjoyed the food, the culture, and the many riads in Marrakech. Their highlights were dining at a restaurant run only by women that served food to die for and exploring the souk, an endless labyrinth of small maze-like covered streets with vendors on both sides, selling everything from collectables to trinkets and clothes. He could almost smell the air there, rich with spices.

He was remembering the main marketplace, Jemaa el-Fnaa, filled with everyone from beggars to snake charmers to gypsy dancers, when the memories lulled him into a doze. But he did not stay in the hubbub of Marrakesh in his dream; he found himself in an elevator going down—first slowly, and then faster and faster. The elevator alarm went off, quietly and then with increasing volume. Max tried to free himself from the elevator, but he was trapped, and the alarm was piercing now...

He awoke from his nightmare with a start and jumped up. He found the cabin lights blinking and several alarms buzzing and beeping loudly.

"What's happening?" he hurriedly called to the captain, who seemed to be having a tough time. Max's adrenalin spiked.

"We have a problem with one of the engines. We hit some geese," said the captain, and he continued to radio for help. "Mayday! Mayday! This is *The Kristoff*. Can anyone hear me?"

The radio crackled and the captain repeated his distress call, with no response.

"This is not looking good, sir. We may need to crash land. Brace yourself, please. I don't think there's any water around and the sun hasn't come up yet. My guess is we're flying somewhere over the northern Himalayas, and this area is full of mountain peaks, so there's a chance we may not find flat ground."

The captain returned to the radio. "Mayday! Mayday! We are losing altitude fast and have lost a lot of fuel. We are losing altitude... I need to take this bird down."

It was almost six a.m. and the sun was not expected to come up for another hour. The captain's visibility was poor.

Max was trying to keep his cool, though his heart was beating at what felt like 300 beats per minute. His life started flashing before his eyes. He saw scenes from his childhood, his teenage years, and his first job. He saw the moment when Aira said yes to his marriage proposal, and when they had their first son. He saw his mother and his brothers.

Max was convinced these were his last moments as the plane plunged downward. The right engine was spewing smoke and flames. He heard Aira's gentle voice in his mind: *Max, I love you.*

"BRACE FOR IMPACT!" shouted the captain.

Max held on, saying a silent prayer of gratitude, waiting...

Kaboom! The loud roar ripped through the aircraft, and Max passed out.

14

KNOW YOURSELF BETTER THAN ANYONE ELSE

Many times in life we face the inevitable: a loss, a catastrophe, a tragedy. Whatever it is, an unpredictable event that disrupts the status quo is hardly ever welcome. Think about it from a personal perspective. A relationship break-up, an argument with a colleague, a disagreement with a friend—all are difficult to handle.

Our response to these situations is based on two things. The first is our core personality, which has developed through our childhood and into adulthood. We may be moved by a simple gesture that brings tears to our eyes, or we may not. Some of us may hold back emotion, believing that to be the best way to react to things. Whether you agree or disagree, there are some things that make us all feel the same, no matter how we react to them.

A smiling baby, a happy dog, a laughing child—these are all things that make us happy. A crying person, an angry friend, a confrontation—these can all make us feel miserable. I am talking about your natural response, which may be completely different to someone else's, depending on your personality.

How do our personalities shape our reactions to the events around us? Have you given a thought to how you react to some common events that happen to you on a daily basis? Are you too absorbed in something to notice beauty or happiness, courage or sadness? *Are you in tune with yourself?* That is the question I am trying to get to, because it may be the most important question you will ask yourself on any given day.

Life can sometimes be unpredictable and throw events in your face that you never expected. How do you expect to bounce back from these events if you don't know who you are? It is unfortunate to see people suffering, knowing that if they had only understood themselves, they could have changed their fate, despite the fact that luck may not be on their side. Luck is something we considered earlier. Can bad luck be invoked by a series of bad steps that get compounded to a negative outcome that is not in your favor? It definitely can.

The biggest quest you can undertake in your life is that of trying to know yourself. Not who you aspire to be or wish you were… who you are. If you want to benefit from your skills and knowledge, then learn about what drives you, what scares you, what you like doing, and how you see the world. Our biggest drawback sometimes is our tendency to neglect ourselves and then expect the world to bend over backwards for us. We do not take the time to see that our own behaviors, actions, and attitudes may have caused the circumstance that we are encountering. When life throws a curveball, and the universe wants to challenge your thoughts and actions, how do you react?

Take the time to understand your motivations. Make an inventory of your skills and experiences, the key turning points in your life, and the lessons learned. This is for you and for nobody else. Know yourself, because you will need to tap into that knowledge in order to make good decisions and judgements almost every day of your life.

15

BAD TIMES ARE ALWAYS INCONVENIENT

It had been over four hours since the airplane crashed into the mountains. Surprisingly, there was no explosion; and thankfully, most of the aircraft was still intact. The dense forest cover had slowed the aircraft as it landed.

Max could not move his arms or legs and barely had the energy to open his mouth and shout for help. He felt like his body was stuck in a tar-like substance that restricted his movement. He could not open his eyes to see where he was, but he could smell pine trees on the breeze and he could hear voices.

"Wala baba, wala yoor."

"Jaldi karu, khabar ha ye kya chu gomut."

Max recognized the dialect but could not make sense of it. He passed out again.

The plane had crashed in a remote valley in the Himalayas—in Kashmir, the land of Max's forefathers. This was a wild landscape, difficult to live on, inhabited by plenty of wildlife—including the prized red stag, the hangul—but few people. Those who lived there were mainly shepherds and gypsies.

The crashed airplane in the valley had been found by Sattar Joo and his young son, Jamal, who were grazing their sheep. They spoke a language not understood by many, a form of Dardic that was indigenous to the region. Sattar and his son did not have modern transportation, and travelled mostly on foot. They did have two horses with them, though.

"Get the horses, Jamal," said Sattar to his son. "This man is hurt. We must hurry and take him to shelter."

It was a cold autumnal morning and the temperatures at that high altitude could sometimes take a devastating plunge. Jamal ran to get the horses, and soon the father and son were heading down the valley to their village, with the unconscious Max laid over a horse.

Sattar summoned the village medicine man. The nearest hospital was two days' walk away, and a bus came only once a week to bring supplies to the small polyclinic in the next village. This was a place without any automation, technology, or modern amenities. Max was far away from home. There was no phone communication, no electricity, and no running water. He was in a place one hundred years behind modern society—and yet he was among his ancestral roots.

Over the next few hours, Sattar Joo and his family made Max comfortable. On the advice of the medicine man, they kept him warm and fed him a combination of herbal teas that Sattar's wife provided. Max was out cold, yet alive. It was going to be a long wait, and everyone prayed that this man who'd fallen out of the sky survived. They prayed for the pilot too, who had not been found.

16

AN UNEXPECTED LANDING

Kashmir is the land of sages and saints. Revered as a beautiful and mystical valley, over the past few thousand years Kashmir has been the envy of many a dynasty, who then conquered it and made it home. Quite recently, the Mughals, the dynasty that ruled the Indian subcontinent, made Kashmir their summer home for at least a few centuries. Their legacy is still seen in Kashmir, in the Mughal gardens and forts created during their time.

Kashmir has a rich cultural heritage, and is home to one of the strongest Buddhist communities in the world. The region attracts greedy nations eager to claim what was never theirs: to the north, China has taken a corner of the country; to the south, India rules half of Kashmir; to the west, Pakistan rules a smaller portion. Since far back in its history, Kashmir has been plundered and ruled by kings who cared less about the people and more about the wealth it generated for them through its rich landscapes and mineral deposits.

Kashmir is also known as the place where Christ found his final home. According to legend, after being resurrected from his tomb, Christ travelled extensively, and ended up settling in Kashmir and spending his last days there. The tomb of Yuz Asaf, in the city of Srinagar, the capital of Kashmir, is believed to be that of Jesus, although no markings support the claim.

But Max knew nothing of this historical place into which he had fallen. Over the next three days, he went in and out of consciousness, while Sattar Joo and his family did their best to reduce his fever and keep him stable. It was fall and the weather had already started turning colder. The nights were much colder than just a few weeks ago, and snowfall was inevitable. Everyone waited and hoped for the best.

On Friday morning, as the Muezzin announced a call for prayer that echoed from the valley below, Max opened his eyes, and for the first time he was able to take in his surroundings. His recollection of events was not quite clear, but he did remember the airplane going down and crashing. His throat was sore and dry, and he wanted a sip of water. He saw a copper jug beside his bed and was slowly trying to reach it when a hand grabbed his. It was

Jamal, the young boy who had been sleeping on the floor right beside the bed.

"Water, water... I give—no move," he said in broken English.

Over the next day, Max regained most of his senses and was able to walk around. Luckily, he had no broken bones, just a concussion, but his body ached all over. He was worried about Aira and what she must be going through, and he wanted to contact her as soon possible. But the closest town was twenty miles down the mountain and he could not summon that level of energy; plus his mind was still a bit foggy.

Sattar and some of the other villagers went back to the crash site, but they were unable to find the pilot. Their best guess was that he had been eaten by wild animals or had possibly been ejected from the plane some distance away. There was simply no way to find out.

Two weeks later, Max had fully recovered from his injuries, and he had got through to Aira on the telephone and reassured her that he was okay. With her support, he had decided to take time off work—take time off everything, in fact—and explore his roots.

Max had become known around the village as The Man Who Fell from the Sky. He could not speak the language, but he fit right in, because he had the same roots. He even looked the part: The Kashmir people have a very distinct look, with their dark hair and tall, muscular build.

Max had spent the past two weeks learning about the village and the surrounding area. He was surprised to find that the village—although cut off from the rest of the world—was self-sustaining. Everything you could need was there: fresh vegetables, fruits, water, livestock. This was a community in its own right. Max had never been in such a place before, and this was the first time he had encountered life with no access to technology.

Max spent time with the village elders, listening to their age-old wisdom and understanding how they worked, what they did for a living, and how the sensitive fabric of their culture had been preserved so well. The history of the village went back to the time of the Mughals, and over the past few hundred years not much had changed.

Max wondered how the villagers were able to raise families and educate their children. He wondered how they could not know what the internet was and how they could live without it. But then, there appeared to be no need for it.

The more Max learned, the more intrigued he became. With the help of Jamal, Max explored the village, which he found to be very clean. People greeted him with a smile, yet maintained a distance.

There was a spirit of friendliness and compassion in the air. The villagers lived a very simple life without modern conveniences, yet their faces glowed with happiness. Again, Max was astounded to see no technology being used—and yet he saw there was no need for it.

He wanted to know the secret of surviving without technology and he asked Sattar how they lived the way they did, and what made everyone in the village so content. Instead of answering the question himself, Sattar suggested Max meet the village council whose weekly meeting would be held that night. Max eagerly looked forward to the gathering.

Later that night, the village quietened down, but there was an air of excitement. The central courtyard in the middle of the village was lit with fire torches placed in a circle formation, and villagers started seating themselves around the circle. Soon, the council members arrived. One by one, they took the center spot and spoke. Max noted that addressing the crowd in a circular fashion helped to create a feeling of community. The talk slowly would down, and the meeting ended with a simple dinner, for which every family in the village contributed one food item. *This is a potluck,* Max thought.

Sattar had arranged a private meeting for Max with the council so that they could have a meaningful conversation.

"We are a simple community, and we were established with a few fundamental principles," said Wali Khan, head of the village elders. "This village has everything we need to sustain us, and it has been this way for the last two hundred years. Many of us go down to the other villages and even to the big city to sell our goods and crops, but we always come back—not because this is the best place to live in the whole world, but because what we have created here is unique."

"But how does everyone not wish to leave because they don't have access to technology and modern facilities?" asked Max.

Wali smiled. "Let me tell you more about us and maybe it will become clear. Our village has a policy: Nobody is permitted to live here unless they agree to the rules first. Everyone is free to leave if they please; we never prevent anyone from leaving. We are not against modernization or technology, and you may be surprised to know that many of us are somewhat in tune with the modern times, although it may not seem that way. But we have made a conscious choice to live as we do, for the sake of preserving our cultural and social fabric."

He continued: "The village is based on some basic rules that are not complicated to follow. More than rules, they are the path that we expect everyone to follow in order to attain the common goal of having the lifestyle that we enjoy. We call them the *axioms of life*. Our forefathers agreed that if we followed these axioms, we would always have a great quality of life, filled with abundance, happiness, and good health. To this day we follow these axioms and impart our values to the next generations.

"We are happy to share these axioms with you, not because you asked, but because the axioms teach us to help others in whatever ways we can. So we have an obligation to share with you everything you want to know."

Max was a bit overwhelmed by the elder's belief in sharing rather than holding back. He could not help but think of the world he came from, where the majority of things were considered private, proprietary; secrets that would not be openly shared with the common people.

This was going to be the lesson of a lifetime for him, because these axioms were going to transform his current way of thinking.

17

THE SEVEN AXIOMS ARE FOUNDATIONAL

The elders agreed to share the axioms with Max, but first they asked him to make them a promise. Max was not expecting this and he asked what the promise was about.

Wali replied: "There is only one promise you need to make, and it is that you will teach these axioms to at least ten more people in your lifetime—the sooner, the better. This knowledge can only be useful when shared. Before we tell you what the axioms are, we need to know you are ready to accept this gift of knowledge."

Max was tuned in to this message and there was nothing else he could think to say but yes. He had come through far too much turmoil to reach the village to reject this offer. He thought maybe his plane had crashed for a reason, and that he was destined to be there and learn the wisdom. Although he was not sure what he was going to learn, his gut told him his life was about to change. He could not have been more correct.

Here are the seven axioms and their application in the modern world.

AXIOM 1

THE KINDEST WORDS AND ACTIONS HAVE NO EQUAL

"The first axiom of life is about kindness, and it has two parts," said Wali, who spoke for the elders.

"The first part is the kindness of words. Every word you speak has an effect on someone. This even includes you. So be careful about what words you bring forth from your mind onto your tongue. Words have the power to move nations and bring tears to the eyes. There is nothing more powerful than a word spoken with meaning and value. So be kind with every word you speak, for you do not know the darkness or light the other person comes from. If they come from a darker place, your words can bring them light and change their world. If they come from a place brighter than yours, then it is an opportunity for you to absorb some of that light and call it your own.

"Speak words that are not false or deceitful. Speak words that are not lies or mocking. Speak not behind the back of your brothers and sisters, and speak not of people, but of things you can do together.

"Words also have the power to recover a soul from the darkest dungeons of hell, and to change a person into a friend. Was it not words that the prophets delivered from their tongues to others, changing the state of nations?

"Be kind with your words in fear and in anger. When in doubt, utter no word, for a word said wrongly can change the fate of the world. Be kind with your words to yourself and say not things that give you shame. You may not be in the right place to say good things, but the darkness in words lingers on and leaves a mark. Be good with your words.

"The second part is to act kindly. Actions are everything we do when we are conscious and for which we can be held to account. Actions are more than touch, and can be related to words that change into actions. Actions help others in a time of need. Help others with your actions when they need you and watch over your neighbors. Actions can build a bridge and feed an empty mouth. Actions can also bring peace and eliminate war. Actions are seeds that you can sow every day to reap the crop of good thoughts tomorrow.

"People have a tendency to define themselves by actions, but the reality is that actions are not the person. They are an extension of their thoughts and how they want to be remembered. Aren't some actions bad, so that they hurt other people or make the lives of others worse? Yes, they are, but they are an extension of the thoughts of a person, not the person themselves. Everyone is born as pure as the divine light of the universe, and yet it is actions that change them in ways unseen.

"Say one good word and do one good action every day."

Max was glued to every word that the elder had spoken, and they made complete sense to him. He had never thought that the wisdom of the village was actually the wisdom of the entire world. He failed to understand what the problem is when the wisdom is available everywhere and yet there are people who do not talk or act the way they should.

Max asked: "Why is there an imbalance between people knowing this and acting on this?"

Wali replied: "It is as you said. Imagine a man standing by a river. How can he cross the river?"

"He can go on the bridge, take a boat, or even swim," Max said with confidence.

"Yes, that's right," said Wali. "But he will not cross the bridge until he does one of these things. It is acting upon his knowledge that will help him to be on the other side, rather than the thought itself. People need to cross."

Max understood. Obviously, execution was the biggest problem for people trying to achieve something. He was listening like a child would listen to a fairy tale, but trying to connect everything to his world, to where he came from, to what he knew. In all his years as an entrepreneur, Max had consistently tried to help people grow as part of his business. Had he done everything he could? He was not sure. There were always things that could be done in a better way. He thought about the modern world and technology, and how despite the advances, technology had created a huge hurdle in having meaningful conversations with people. Not just in the workplace, but everywhere. How many times, he thought, did he stop and speak to a homeless person, and ask them how they were and whether he could do something for them? For that matter, he could think of anything he did consistently to help others because of a value.

Max was privileged to be living the life he was living, and now, so many hundreds of miles away, saved by a people he did not know yet from whom he was descended, he was learning a life lesson. It was all a bit overwhelming. Life was no coincidence, and it was no coincidence that he was there with the elders under the starry night.

"Where I come from," he said to the elders, "we seldom use words for comfort, but to get things done. The way we speak to others is less about compassion and more about need. We need more from everyone, and we barely think of the effect of our words on others. I feel that with the world developing so fast, we are breaking down what it means to be human and connect to others. If it is words that connect us to others, then not using them the right way is not right at all. It bothers me to think about what we need to change."

The elders smiled, and Wali answered: "You are not the first person in the world who is seeing or saying this. Many before you have raised the point. The fact that the world is changing is not new. The world has been changing as long as the human race has existed. It changed from hundreds of thousands of years ago at the time of the early man, to the dynasties like those in Egypt and Samarra. It changed with the Incas and those in Asia. The world is constantly changing, and that's why we need to adapt to it and preserve ourselves.

"Through the ages, the wisdom that has been passed down across civilizations, the wisdom of wise men and prophets, has collectively conveyed very basic messages. This is one of those messages, and to make it a reality, you have to make sure that you consciously say one good thing to someone and do one good deed for someone every day. You have to do this consciously, and also acknowledge that you performed this action. This is the seed you will be planting every day.

"Think about your family, friends, and colleagues. These are all human relationships, and more than money, things, and transactions, what matters is how you connect with these people in your life. Imagine sowing a seed and watering it to see it grow. The next day, you realize that someone else watered it and exposed it to sunshine, and now the plant is bigger. The next day, you see that someone else tended to the soil and removed the weeds, and the plant is now growing faster. This is the effect that occurs when we all vibrate at the same frequency and nourish the seeds of good that together we have planted and tended. It is a human tendency to encourage the good and to respect it when someone else does good for us. You will see the kindness coming back to you in multiple ways; you will see it return tenfold. That is the effect of doing something good, one thing at a time, every day."

Max loved the idea. When he thought about his world and all the technology, he realized he could perhaps use it to communicate this axiom. After all, for him technology was a mechanism, a tool to create results, and quickly. More than ever, he wanted to do something that combined this new knowledge and his skills. His mind was busy making connections.

Within a customer-focused world, we often want to make a connection between the theories of getting results and the way we work. This axiom can be applied to any workplace or business situation by making it part of the company culture.

There is a famous story about someone utilizing this axiom to create positive change. A technical support guy was speaking to a lady from the helpdesk at the provider company. They were trying to figure out how to fix an issue. It was almost dinnertime and the technician on the customer side asked his colleague if he was hungry, and suggested maybe they should order pizza. The vendor rep overheard this and took the opportunity to make an impact on her customer and genuinely do something good. She ordered a pizza delivery. Imagine the customer's surprise when the pizza guy rang the bell on the other side of the country! The customer and the vendor ended up fixing the problem, both left the interaction with a positive result, and the lady's kind gesture would be remembered forever. This is an example of someone utilizing the first axiom to go above and beyond the call of duty.

Max wanted to adopt this axiom for the modern world, and not just get it across to his organization but to others too, including his customers and partners. So he wrote down the following note:

Communicate a positive to someone every day.

Doing this is not difficult for anyone if they take the time and consciously communicate a positive idea, thought, or comment to someone—a co-worker, partner, employee, team member, or customer. The idea is to start small, with something that anyone can do.

Max was a well-informed and knowledgeable leader, and he knew that people work well with a reward in mind and that sometimes a gentle nudge goes a long way to motivate people. He wanted to inspire people to take this action, but did not know how. He wanted to do more than just offer financial rewards. He wanted to do something else, but he could not think of anything immediately.

The elders and Max were served hot saffron tea and a traditional savory bread from Kashmir called *kulcha*. As Max ate and drank, he could not wait to hear more from these wise men.

AXIOM 2

PAY YOUR DEBT TO YOURSELF

"The second axiom of life that we follow is very personal to everyone," said Wali. "We owe it to ourselves to be good to ourselves. This means taking care of two things: the body and the mind."

"First, we have a responsibility to take care of our bodies. We often get too busy to take good care of the one thing that is precious to us all, but we must. We must eat healthy and nourishing foods, those that are in season.

"In the past, every grain we ate was grown in our backyards, so to speak. We ate the fruits, vegetables, and crops we grew, and we ate meat from the herds we raised, always taking as much as we wanted and never more than we needed. This is because we have to strike a balance between what is abundant and what is scarce, between what is flourishing and what is dying. The body is the haven for the mind, and if we fail to keep the body in a healthy condition, the mind will not function in the right way. For this reason, even now we try to raise our own crops and eat from what the valley and the forest provide. For every tree we cut down, we make sure to plant two more, and for every cow we sacrifice, we make sure to rear two more. This was the way of our forefathers and we continue this tradition. The village is self-sufficient; we do not need to get anything from outside. In fact, we maintain very little contact with the outside world, and try to raise our own crops and animals. As a result, it is not uncommon for people in the village to live a long, healthy life. Even in old age, our people look younger than they are and have energy, vigor, and vitality."

Max was perplexed to hear that none of the supplies in the village came from outside, because he had seen all kinds of fresh produce in the small marketplace that served the community.

"How do you support the whole village? Don't you fall short?" asked Max.

"We only take what we need," said Wali. "We do not waste food, we do not kill in excess, and we do not grow to throw. This is the balance we have been maintaining. Right from when our children are born, we teach them these values by taking them to the fields where we work and making them part of the process. This way they understand where food comes from and how much energy and nurturing every crop needs to be turned into something we eat. Our new generations are the keepers of this tradition, and if we do not enable them and make them understand how this tradition works, we cannot expect to preserve it."

Max pondered the fact that over one third of the food we produced in the West went to waste. That was such a catastrophe when millions of people on the planet were hungry. Despite the fact that we had technologically advanced as a race, we seemed to have forgotten some key lessons in preserving the world. In the so-called modern societies, Max thought, food was something that was picked from a shelf and not from a tree. Our children needed a lesson in how real sustainability worked. He thought about what Wali had said. He realized that unless we took part in teaching our children these values, we ourselves would not learn what needed to be done, and so we could not expect someone else to do it in the future.

Something had to change. Max thought about ideas he would implement at work, and how even a small program to eliminate food waste could help shift people's mindset. It was not saving the actual food that was important so much as changing people's mindset to help eliminate the problem at the root. He had hope.

Wali continued: "The second aspect of paying our debt to ourselves is to take care of the mind. The human mind is one of the most amazing things in the world. Unlike animals, we are capable of so many things, such as expression, creativity, and ingenuity. What we think can help all of mankind. If you look at the world around you, you should realize that everything you see is the result of someone else thinking about something and creating it. Every invention and innovation was once an idea.

"The mind is also able to come up with solutions to very complex problems. Think about all the doctors who use the collective knowledge of the science of medicine to treat diseases and heal the sick. This is a result of humans opening doors for others, and what better way to succeed than help others and live life in the service of others?

"But the mind is also very sensitive. The mind is controlled by what we think and how we think, and because of that we sometimes have thoughts that do not benefit anyone—thoughts that are born of anger or sickness. We have to take care of the mind so that we do not focus on the negative, but instead on the positive and our ability to make changes to the world and to help everyone around us.

"When both body and mind are in synchronization with each other, you reach a state of optimal living and peace, something we all strive for. We believe in thinking about the positive, talking about positive outcomes, encouraging our young ones with positive words, and even discussing the biggest challenges in a positive light. Everything that happens in this world creates a reaction in one form or another, and the wisdom of our forefathers has proved time and again that a positive mindset has the greatest effect."

Max could not help but laugh, because the world he came from was a very different one. Taking care of your mind had become a business. People were addicted to drugs as recreation. And the idea of a sound mind was far-fetched in the corporate world, which was full of stress, tension, and the hunger to make more money. People were driven financially, and by thoughts of what they could have and what others had that they did not. It was a world where money was king, and a sound mind was far down your list of priorities.

But it should not be that way, and there must be a way to break down this barrier. Max wrote down on his sheet of paper:

Every day, do one thing that helps your health and one thing that helps your mind.

He thought about what would fit into this. Reading a book, taking a power walk, listening to a self-development tape, or watching a self-development video. In the age of technology there were so many options. Max wanted his friends, family, and employees to adopt this principle, and more than anything he wanted them to benefit. But who would be accountable for this? He always wanted to close the loop with accountability in place. Why not make developing people a part of the workplace, he thought, rather than a thing they needed to do? Max knew he had a lot of work ahead.

AXIOM 3

EDUCATE A PERSON TO GIVE BIRTH TO A NATION

Wali continued with the third axiom. This was an axiom all about the power of knowledge.

"The third axiom is the imperative to gain and spread knowledge. Had it not been for humans acquiring knowledge of different things, there would be no difference between us and animals. For this reason, knowledge has been a pillar of our existence.

"In the past, our forefathers learned about things such as crops, health, and medicines, and they preserved this knowledge in books and by teaching it to each new generation. This knowledge is a source we can tap into whenever we need.

"The axiom says that educating even one person is equal to giving birth to a nation. Is it not true that every nation in history has had a leader who went above and beyond his or her call of duty to lead the nation to success? Leaders are not leaders because they were born that way, but because of the knowledge they possess. The ability to learn and use information is key in helping us progress as a race. Today, knowledge is available via many means, and that is why the world can be a much better place than it has been, but it all depends on how that knowledge and information is used."

Max could not relate this to his own life situation. He thought that with the internet, all the information was in the hands of people to utilize. People had access to so much information that they could use to better their lives and the lives of others. But that was not what really happened. He knew of people who wasted time learning things that did not add any value. Children of all ages wasted time watching videos and speaking to their friends on their modern devices, when they could be learning something new that would help them and others in so many different ways.

Back in the day, passing on knowledge was something that started with the birth of a child. By age ten children were already accomplished in history, and the art of war or strategy. Some children were also working with their fathers and mothers in the fields, growing crops and preserving their family traditions while learning important lessons about life.

Then Max's thoughts turned to all the people in the world who did not have the privilege of knowledge. People who were uneducated, who did not go to school. People who had no special knowledge beyond what life had taught them. There was a great opportunity ahead that we could work on.

"Knowledge helps preserve the sanity of nations," continued Wali. "It is the biggest reason for peace. With knowledge, nations do not wage war on others, but instead engage in the intellectual exchange of ideas and work on how to solve problems together. People do not fight for small things or big ones, because they realize that the biggest possession they have is knowledge and that the only way to grow it is to share it. It is this thinking that makes nations great and makes people a source of change for the greater good.

"How many wars have happened in recent times that could have been averted? How many people have been killed for the sake of money, land, or precious minerals? How many children, women, and men have been made homeless because two nations could not agree on who keeps the land, and yet they displace the most precious thing they could have as a nation, its people and their minds? How many skilled people who possess knowledge that is so precious it would take decades to learn have been displaced because their lands did not value their contributions and art? It is the lack of human knowledge that causes war, and no matter how you look at it, the lack of an intellectual exchange of ideas is the root cause of much of the pain, suffering, and tragedy in the world. We can solve all of this with the exchange of knowledge.

Max considered how the business world perceived knowledge, and how there was so much opportunity to help people grow and share that knowledge with others. Building a knowledge bank prepares us for the future, and it goes beyond small things. Knowledge, as the saying goes, is power, and when the right knowledge is learned and shared, it creates a wave of change.

Max thought about the countless wars that had been fought in the last hundred years—the two world wars and the many smaller, regional wars in which scores had been killed and millions displaced; the brutal killings in Africa, and the countless cases of genocide in Europe and other places where communities were targeted and systematically killed. Max was almost in tears as he thought about the recent civil wars in places such as Rwanda, Iraq, Syria, and Somalia. The tears came when his thoughts turned to all the mothers who had seen their children dying before them and the hundreds of children who were orphaned, just because of someone's thinking.

If only we could possess the knowledge of how to change the state of the world.

AXIOM 4

WE ARE PART OF MULIPLE FAMILIES

"The idea of family is very different for everyone," Wali said. "For some, family means people that are immediately related to you, like your parents, children, and siblings. For others, family includes extended family and maybe even friends. In the village, we use our internal value system to determine whom we call family. It is the way you want to treat people that determines whether they are family or not, rather than you expecting a certain treatment from them. Ultimately, family means being able to support others in a time of need, such as ill health. Family also means ensuring family members' wellbeing. What would be the value of family if you did not look out for your family members and wish them well? It would defeat the purpose.

"It is important to understand that a family is always made from different building blocks that fit together, and for these blocks to fit, you need to have the blocks in the first place. Every individual is a block, and they form part of the family. For you to benefit from this mechanism of family and help others benefit too, you have to valuable, by doing your best to utilize your abilities. This does not mean you have to be rich. It means that unless you are on the journey to self-empowerment and actualization, you may not be able to function well as a unit within any family.

"As one person, you are a fundamental building block in your family, and hence taking care of yourself is very important. You have to treat yourself the right way and build upon the axioms to feel good physically and mentally. Only then can you serve the needs of the family. If you are the head of the family then you owe it to the other members of that family to be the best version of yourself, despite the flaws and weaknesses you have, and to keep the benefit and safety of the family in mind. When you are part of a family and other members depend on you, your decisions have to make complete sense to them, because you are the one who controls many factors that affect the family.

"Think about it this way. When all the wheels on a cart work well and in unison, the cart moves forward. When a back wheel is broken, the front wheels can still move the cart and carry the load until the cart can be fixed. But when the front wheel is broken, it is more difficult to move the cart, and it puts a lot more stress on the remaining wheels and the animal that pulls it.

"When you expand the idea of family to your neighborhood or your village, you have more members and your duties expand to consider these extended family members as well. You become a guide and a shepherd, gathering these members to impart knowledge and teach skills they can use. You also become a beacon of light for the family and are looked upon with respect by all.

"Extend this to the city and the country you live in, and the family now has many people who take responsibility for imparting their knowledge and helping to keep the family safe. They teach new things, teaching from experience, and help to build a strong community. Now expand this idea to the entire world, and we can have a global family, in which the key elements of respect, admiration, learning, and safety occur naturally.

"This is how the idea of the family starts with you and ends with the world. Wouldn't it be nice to live in a world where we can trust each other and build a better world as a global family?"

Max was astonished at the depth of this wisdom and the ideology behind it. This was no different from the wisdom of Lao Tzu, the Chinese saint revered as the father of philosophy, and that of Rumi, the mystic who changed the world with his thoughts on universal love.

"How did we miss the boat?" asked Max. "Why aren't we able to adhere to these ideas in the modern world?"

"Perhaps the answer lies in the fact that when people are too distracted by other things, they lose track of what is actually important," replied Wali.

It was almost midnight, yet Max was feeling energized. His conversation with the elders was enlightening and thought-provoking. He was getting a life lesson in one of the most magical places he had ever traveled to (well, in this case, dropped in on).

He asked the elders: "How do we then connect ourselves to the world we live in? I come from a place where everything needs to be done in the least amount of time, and there is a scarcity of resources, such as gasoline to run our cars. I'm trying to make sense of how to connect everything together."

Wali replied: "You need to understand all of the axioms to make a complete circle. Let me tell you about the fifth axiom, which may help answer your question."

AXIOM 5

SUSTENANCE WILL SUFFICE WHEN THE FOREST LIVES

"We live in the forest," said Wali, "and it is a big source of sustenance in our lives. In a typical forest, you have many types of plants, ranging from the ones that bear flowers to those that bear fruit. You also have plants that grow under the ground and whose roots provide sustenance, and still others that provide us with wood to make our homes.

"The forest in all its glory is a living, breathing organism that is made up of countless elements, all of which have specific life cycles. Take a look at the ants that live within the forest. They live in colonies underground that have a complex hierarchy; they are one of the best examples of a complex society that works with 100 percent efficiency. The ants all have predetermined tasks, and they perform these tasks in the best possible way they can.

"We also have other small animals in the forest, such as bees, wasps, and termites, and they have their own tasks to perform and roles to play. At a larger level, we have animals that do their predetermined jobs and maintain the equilibrium in the forest, like the predators, which cull the populations of other animals as needed. The animal kingdom is hence balanced within the forest, with each species making its own unique contribution.

"All of these things within the forest give us humans sustenance as well as shelter. But when this balance is disturbed, everything gets disrupted. Our forefathers devised the fifth axiom to convey that maintaining this balance is essential for our survival, because we depend on the forest for our very existence.

"Today the world is changing dramatically and fewer people think of the forest as a provider. Many get their food from big stores, for example. But the balance is still essential. When the sources of foods are gone and the forest is no more, where will we humans go to seek sustenance? The forest serves as a symbol that stands for everything in nature. Be it trees, plants, animals, water, earth, or any other naturally existing element, the forest represents them all. When we cut down a tree and we do not plant two more in its place, the balance is disturbed. When we kill animals to fill our shelves with excess meat, even if the smallest amount gets wasted, the balance is disturbed. When we build cities and fail to plant more forests to give us the air we breathe, the balance is disturbed."

Max could not agree more with this axiom, because he knew people took the environment for granted. The idea of preserving the environment was not new, but was a time-old tradition in many cultures—from the Americas, where the natives took only what they wanted from the land, to the East, where worshipping nature was a deeply rooted practice.

"How did we fail to get this right?" he asked. "How can we be modern and yet at the same time cause the destruction of millions of acres of forests? This is not the way."

"You are right, this is not the way," said Wali. "But humanity cannot live back in primitive times and sometimes the balance shifts. Time will always put pressure on us to do things differently, but we need to create a balance by offsetting those changes with our conscious efforts. There is no reason we cannot use any of the first five axioms and derive some knowledge from them to help. Why not gain and spread the knowledge we need to be able to preserve the environment? Or treat the environment as a part of our family so that we care for it? The axioms work with each other. Following the path the axioms lay out is not easy, but it is the right path and we need to recognize that by being truthful to ourselves in every way.

"The environment we live in sustains us, and if we fail to preserve it, we cannot expect to thrive."

AXIOM 6

HELP OTHERS GET TO WHERE THEY WANT TO BE

"The first five axioms deal with personal growth and actions that address internal challenges," Wali went on. "All of these are key in how we take care of ourselves and how we manage our relationships. The sixth axiom is about giving. Unlike the first five axioms, this axiom specifically talks about helping others.

"You may say, 'How can I help others? I do not have anything to give others.' The answer lies in giving what you have. This is not about giving money, or a tangible item. It is about helping people to achieve their goals. Everyone around is seeking something: health, wealth, knowledge, trust, companionship, and many other things. Through the knowledge that we have gained over the years and our life experiences, we can help people get to where they want to be. But we sometimes don't know our own capabilities and how we can help others.

"Imagine that you own a forest—it is yours to keep. This forest is spread over hundreds of acres of land. It contains many plants, trees, animals, and other natural wonders. The forest keeps on growing every day; new shoots push through the ground and new flowers bloom. If you wanted to, you could fill hundreds of books with the names and uses of all the plants and trees in your forest.

"Because the forest is yours, you have a fence surrounding it that keeps people out. Leading from the only gate in the fence is a path that connects this forest to the outside world. Many a time, a traveler ends up at the gate and seeks your permission to enter. They want to see what is inside and maybe gather some plants. Cutting the plants down does not do damage, as they grow back quickly, and the plants can be used in all sorts of beneficial ways. Some people find peace while walking through the forest as you guide them, telling them about the plants. Some people benefit just by looking at one plant and then leaving. Others are regular visitors to your forest, enjoying its beauty and becoming good friends with you.

"This is exactly how the mind works and how our life experiences help others. Our life is like the forest and our experiences are like the plants. These experiences can help others in many ways—

ways we cannot even guess sometimes. Experiences that you have had over a lifetime are the biggest source of inspiration to some, and you should never underestimate the importance of what you can bring to the lives of others.

"Your help isn't needed only when people need to achieve a fixed goal. Many times you will be approached by people who do not have a fixed goal, and you can help them to determine their goal and derive meaning from their lives.

"Philosophers from different parts of the world have characterized this helpfulness in different ways. Some people associate helping others with religion; but in all honesty, religion has nothing to do with helping others and everything to do with being human."

Max asked: "In my world, people look after themselves and protect themselves first, before helping others. So what benefit would this axiom bring to people?"

"Good question," said Wali. "The answer is that giving to others brings a great deal of benefits. Follow this axiom, and you are aligning with the first five axioms too."

Max thought about the other axioms and how they connected. Helping others tied in with being kind to others. It also connected to imparting knowledge to others, and preserving the sense of family by seeing the people you helped as your extended global family. Helping others would definitely bring overall good to the world and contribute to changing the way people thought about the environment. This axiom would help people in so many ways that it was unimaginable.

This was one of the greatest learning experiences for Max, as he thought of all the ways he could turn this wisdom around and create change in his world.

AXIOM 7

OWN YOUR GRATITUDE— IT'S YOURS

Time had flown, and it was almost early morning now. The fire was still burning and Max, although tired, was keen to hear more. He felt as if he was at a transformative point in his life.

Wali continued: "The last axiom binds all the axioms together, just like a thread binds together the beads of a rosary and makes it complete. Gratitude is key to living a life of abundance. It is so important that if you fail to follow this axiom in your life, all the work you do on the other axioms may just be wasted.

"Gratitude is the act of thanking the Creator, God, whatever you believe runs the universe: the environment, the forests, the oceans, us. Philosophers have often said that we are part of the universe in such a close way that we and everything else are made from the same raw material. This means the sun and the moon, the oceans and the lakes, the forests and the deserts, and even people are all composed of the same basic raw material. So we are part of Creation, and in our lives we have more abundance than we can ever imagine.

"Think about your life right now. Forget the problems you may be facing, the issues you want to resolve, and the goals you want to achieve. You have come to the point now where you have made countless decisions, and journeyed from your past to the present moment. Your experiences in life are not a matter of chance, but built by you, through your decisions and the opportunities you have taken.

"If you start thinking from a mindset of gratitude, you will see that everything you have done in life so far and everything you possess is what you wished for at some stage in your life and then achieved. The achievement was probably very important to you at that stage. Perhaps you worked very hard to achieve something that seemed so important that you could fight the world for it. It could be a job that you wanted badly, or a home, or good health. It could be anything. Now, two things are possible. The first is that you still love those things, and now that you possess them you appreciate having them. The second is that you are so used to those things now, you hardly even notice them. These things are around you, but you have taken them for granted, and maybe do not even like them now.

"The way you think about things is your responsibility. If the importance of something in your life increases or decreases, that is on you and nobody else. The gratitude mindset works in both of these cases: You not only offer thanks for having these things, but—more importantly—you give yourself the credit that you deserve for having achieved these things.

Gratitude is like pouring water to quench someone else's thirst. You never run out of water in your jug. The more you are grateful for, the more your life fills up with abundance. Once you tune yourself in to being grateful, you attract the right things in your life and do not feel miserable about things that are not going well.

"People sometimes mistake positive-minded people for people who are happy for no reason. That is not correct. More than anything, positive people are grateful for the abundance, the opportunities, and the life experiences that make them who they are and make them unique in every aspect. Of the seven billion plus people in the world, every one of us is unique in the experiences we have; and more than that, even though experiences can sometimes be similar, it is our unique mindset that differentiates us from others.

"Your gratitude can go to any level, and there is no limit. You will never increase gratitude to the extent that it is too much. There is no way to have too much gratitude. Remember, the more gratitude you express for yourself, your life, your life experiences, and the force that shapes the universe, the more abundance you will experience in your life."

Max could not agree more. Although he had always found a way to thank the Creator for things he had, he knew sometimes circumstances got the better of him; he was human, after all.

He asked: "How can we adopt all of these axioms in life?"

"That is a question for later," said Wali. "It is morning, and you should rest. You have been through a lot."

Max was mentally exhausted after the events of this night. He retired and fell asleep within seconds. He dreamed of his childhood and his mother, and then of being waist high in crystal-clear waters, surrounded by beautiful, colorful stingrays. Max was finally resting after his ordeal and was at peace with himself.

18

THE SEVEN AXIOMS IN THE BOARDROOM

Max returned home after his long visit with the elders full of inspiration. He took two weeks out to spend time with Aira, before returning to work. His staff and friends were happy to see him back and apparently doing well. There was even a celebration at company headquarters to welcome him back.

Over the next few months, Max re-integrated himself into work and got back to being an excellent leader who knew where to drive the organization. He talked to Aira and his top staff about the ideas he had learned from the elders, and everyone liked the axioms. But over time, things got busy, and Max and the rest of the staff fell back into the usual work routine.

Then came the day when the American people would choose their new leader. It had been an exciting few months leading up to the election, with different candidates wooing the people, showing the best of what they brought to the table and how Americans would benefit from their policies, if elected. It had been a very close race between two candidates who had drastically opposing views.

By evening, it looked like the more conservative candidate would be elected, and American would get a leader focused on fewer changes but long-term stability. It was nine p.m. when breaking news reports announced that a coup had taken place in China, and the political situation was destabilized. China was a strong nation and this was unbelievable news. Catastrophic, in fact.

Max was very concerned about the implications this would have on Rickshaw, Inc., given that more than half of their $1 billion revenue came from ecommerce partners in China. Max called an emergency meeting with his leadership team, and they connected to their office in Asia to assess the situation.

"It is not looking good. We don't know where the situation will go," said Xian Ji, Max's senior vice-president for operations in Asia. "The stock market has crashed, and we have a military crackdown across major cities. This has never happened here before, so we don't know what this will do to business. Right now, we are afraid there may be a long wait before the situation is resolved."

This crisis would have a detrimental effect across the world. Max had a good idea of what the implications would be for Rickshaw. Their revenue projections would tank instantly, and their investors would need reassurances that their money was safe. But if they were lucky, they would find a way to weather this storm before it took the entire ship down.

Max and his team worked on a recovery plan. He wanted to determine the best way to come out of this crisis and he leveraged the help of all his staff in coming up with ideas.

"We need more ideas. Can we shift the revenue projection from Asia to other regions? What is the fastest way to do this?" he asked.

As his teams scrambled about over the next few days, it looked like the global economy was about to face a harsh reality. As a result of the coup, markets around the world had destabilized. Two of the major global stock exchanges had crashed, and while NASDAQ was holding, it had traded as low as had been seen in over a decade. Billions of dollars were being turned into dust, while mass hysteria was hitting investor circles. Smaller companies such as Max's were feeling the pain more than the large companies, because they did not have enough cash reserves to survive a burnout. This was a combination of the dot-com bubble bursting and the big financial crisis of 2008 all over again.

There was little chance that this crisis would resolve itself, and Max had to make a tough choice. He was no longer driven by financial results, and his thinking had dramatically changed after he had returned from his trip. What mattered to him most was the responsibility he felt to support his employees. He knew his employees—some of whom had been with him for years—had obligations, like families. He also knew that when good people faced challenges and they were cornered, it was not good for the families. Turbulence in one part of the world was causing ripples in other places. People were financially vulnerable and may be unable support their families and meet their commitments in such difficult times.

"I think I need to do something bigger than I've ever done," he said to Aira. "What can I do, though?"

Max did not sleep properly for days. As the political situation unfolded, markets did stabilize, yet continued to trade lower. Business was becoming steadier, and thankfully it seemed that it may be possible to come out of this without too much damage.

Two months passed, and things had turned out much better than anticipated. The political situation in China had calmed under a new regime. Global markets had settled down and business was looking bullish. Max had lost more than 28 percent of his company value due to the crash, and yet they had survived the worst.

It was almost the end of the year, and Max decided to hold a meeting with all of his employees. He wanted to address everyone and discuss how the year had ended up, and set the tone for what was to come next year. Invitations were sent, and teams were coordinated.

19

WHAT LIFE IS ALL ABOUT

As Max walked onto the stage, he knew many eyes were upon him. Along with those in the hall, there were employees and friends of the company logged on via web conferencing around the world—over 20,000 people in total, he reckoned. Despite his calm demeanor, Max was anxious. He had a lot to say, and he really wanted his audience to be inspired by his words.

"Good morning, everyone. I am more than pleased to be here today to talk to you. As you know, this year has been full of excitement, and challenges. We started the year by going public, which made a huge impact on how we do business and what we stand for. We proved to ourselves and our customers that we are here to stay, and that our services are not just a one-time sale, but the start of a relationship where the customer's needs are key."

Max went on to talk about how they had performed, what the company had achieved, and what their future plans were, covering all aspects of the business. Then, with the last quarter of his time remaining, Max decided to make the announcements he had been anxiously waiting to make. He had thought about this for many months, and discussed it with Aira, and he was very sure that this would be the biggest step he had taken so far in his journey as an entrepreneur.

Max's experiences throughout the year had been unlike anything that had happened to him before. Surviving the plane crash and spending time in the village had changed his perspective. Over the last few months, he had not spoken much about what he had gone through, but quietly he had been planning a series of dramatic changes, all of which were related to his experiences. Until now, the only people at the company who knew about the changes were his financial advisors, and they had seemed pretty bewildered. But Max was sure this was the right path to take.

"We are making some big changes in the company," he announced to his audience, "from changing the way we work, to changing why we do what we do. These changes are not happening because something dramatic has occurred, or because the market is forcing us to do this. We are making changes because, through some of my recent experiences, I have acquired information that must change our lives.

"You see, we are all living a life, but we are not necessarily living the life we *want*. We live every day in a reactive way. We start reacting to things first thing in the morning, when we check our emails and respond without a thought. *Things just need to be done... I need to send those documents... someone has asked for more of this or that.* We are in a reactive mode 99 percent of the time. And we live like automated machines that are programmed to do certain tasks, and when we are done, we go back to our mobile phones and computers, to be lost in an endless playlist of videos, movies, and other things that take our attention away from what is most important: us!

"We are privileged to be living in a country where we have everything available and accessible, and enjoy a better physical quality of life than 98 percent of the rest of the world. I say *physical* because that's all it amounts to. We have physical comforts— food, resources, and things that keep us busy—and yet our mental quality of life has suffered over the years. We have less time to spend with family and friends, less time to talk about the problems we can solve together and to change the conditions for all the unprivileged people in the world.

"This needs to change. It needs to change not because someone has a problem with it, but because it is the right thing to do. We owe it to ourselves to give ourselves the best options in life, and to create change that affects others in a good way. For this reason, I am here with a plan to change our lives in a meaningful way, to make changes that will affect you more than you could ever imagine."

Everyone in the audience was silent and still, eyes glued to Max. He had grabbed their attention, and they were keen to hear more and to absorb every piece of information he provided.

"We are going to change the mission of our company and our values. These will be things that affect actual work every day, not just posters that we hang on the wall. Unless we are able to put the missions and values into practice, we cannot get the benefit from them.

"We are going to be the world's first company that works *for* its employees, who in turn serve the needs of the customers. We will create an atmosphere in which each of us is treated in the best possible way. In doing so, we may become the envy of the world, and it will be up to us to translate that into a meaningful thing for us and the people we affect.

"Starting next year, we will based our work on seven fundamental values. These will determine our direction, goals, and achievements. They will create meaning in our lives and help us change the world, quite literally.

"I have spent the last few months shaping these core values from the knowledge I gained as a result of my life experiences this year. I've spent countless hours working to make sure these values are actionable and will result in a colossal shift in the lives of the people at this company, the people we serve, and the wider world."

The audience members were surprised, but a sense of happiness was evident on faces. Max had done what nobody expected, and laid the foundations for an organization that really cared about its people and their lives, rather than working them into the ground.

Max had completely shifted the way he saw work. He did not want work to be a drudge, something people did only because they had to make a living. The seven axioms had changed Max's way of looking at things from the perspective of value creation. He knew that all the technology we used had nothing to do with how people functioned and met their basic needs.

PART 2

20

THE SEVEN AXIOMS APPLIED

The internet age has created many new paradigms. Since the dot-com bubble alone there have been thousands of success stories, and more failures than we could count. Through numerous surveys, studies, and conversations, experts have found many insights into what delivers success and how successful companies are formed and sustained— strong leadership, good habits, the overall convergence of teamwork, market timing, and many other factors. It is hard to pinpoint exactly the reasons for success, because there are so many. But a few ideas stand out above the rest. These are ideas that are proven to help people reach their goals and achieve success.

Here is a breakdown of these seven axioms of value creation, the pillars of a successful, world-class organization that creates value for everyone.

AXIOM 1

COMMUNICATION, COLLABORATION, AND GOODNESS

For anyone keen to succeed in business, it goes without saying that communication is key. Communication within the business context happens internally and externally.

Internal communication

Managers at every level must know the value of optimal communication. More than just communicating in an efficient manner, every business *must* be able to create value through communication, saving time, effort, and energy by communicating in a structured and positive manner.

There are countless books about internal stakeholder communication that include guidance on how to manage teams, how to work in a team, how to optimize team communications, and more. All kinds of resources are available, from sources such as communication experts and associations, that focus on helping create a positive flow of communication. Managers and the modern technology workforce should utilize these resources to add value to their work and to create a better work environment.

Here are some key questions to consider:

- Does your organization have an internal communication plan?

- Is this plan reactive or proactive?

- Do you communicate internally to inform or to engage?

- What kind of metrics have you enabled to optimize internal communication?

- Do you have team-building activities in place?

- Does your organization offer structured training and skill-building courses to employees?

- How much did you spend on communications training in the last year?

It goes without saying that efficient teams are able to make better decisions and work in a more productive manner.

In 2014, Gallop conducted a survey that revealed a majority of communications within organizations took place over text, phone, and email. Is your organization using all these mediums for internal communication?

Other industry surveys, such as one carried out by CareerBuilder, show that email is considered to be one of the biggest productivity killers. Is email the primary channel of internal communication for your organization? If yes, are you open to considering other channels that create more engagement? If yes, are you looking into this?

If internal efficiency is not on your radar, then your organization is like the many others that focus on what is ahead and pay little attention to excelling. That's like an Olympic swimmer trying to just swim and win the race without taking the time to perfect their stroke and stamina. Bad move!

External communication

For the sake of this argument, we are going to consider all kinds of external communications. This includes your marketing collateral, press releases, and social media interactions. The question to evaluate is: What is the reason for your external communications?

Take the example of your marketing collateral. What is the one thing that any marketing collateral has to do really well? Sell? Promote? Show capabilities or features? There are many answers to this simple yet key question. Depending upon what you are selling, who will use it, and where will it be utilized, there could be hundreds of different scenarios in every case. Despite the diversity of the answers, there is one common golden thread between every type of marketing, and that is to be able to do this: *Communicate value!*

Communicating value goes beyond just looking at features and how they can be useful. That's just the small stuff. Here are some questions to ask:

- How does your organization communicate value to prospects and customers through marketing communication?

- How much of your marketing communication is about product features?

- How much emphasis in your marketing collateral is on communicating value?

- How much research does your team do on customer profiles to create custom collateral per persona?

- Do you use a persona-based approach to design the collateral roadmap for your customers?

- How specific do you get when talking about business problems with customers?

- How much engagement does your communication create?

These and many other questions start the discussion about creating effective external communications. In this example, we have only talked about marketing collateral. Do a similar exercise with all external communication and look at how it can be optimized. The more specific you get, the better your results.

Use the first axiom to focus your communications strategy and ensure that all your communication establishes a two-way dialogue that transfers and creates value.

AXIOM 2

WHEN PRACTICED AT EVERY LEVEL, ACCOUNTABILITY LEAVES NO ROOM FOR FAILURE

We are not even going to debate whether accountability is necessary for success or not. It is such a key area for getting results that it cannot be underestimated at any cost.

Accountability is also a fundamental building block for trust; not just with other people, but with yourself. If you are accountable to yourself, you will hold yourself to the standards you have set for yourself. Being accountable to others creates an unparalleled environment and relationships that bring a tremendous amount of rewards and success.

A prerequisite to making people accountable in an organization is to empower them. It's like making sure you have the right gear before you go fishing, and only then can you question why or why not you were able to catch fish. Or say you are the captain of a soccer team and you want to win all the matches you play; then you need to make sure that every member of your team at least has the right shoes to be able to compete in a fair way.

Within corporate environments, when you empower people and hold them accountable, value creation occurs. Let us look at a few questions that may open up the discussion to more ideas:

- Apart from a yearly performance review, what mechanisms do you have in place to enable accountability across the board?

- How do you empower your employees?

- What have you done in the last year to help employees show accountability?

- Do you have an internal program that helps employees understand accountability?

- Where is your biggest challenge in accountability within the organization?

They say that if you cannot measure it, you cannot manage it. But how do you measure accountability? What is the unit you use to measure it and how can you track it? Here are some ways to measure accountability at a high level:

- Empower responsible people.

- Create an internal accountability check that connects business metrics.

- Create a culture of accountability, which really works well from the top down.

- Build trust between your employees and teams.

- Help people embrace accountability by incentivizing it.

How do leaders follow this process for creating accountability within their organizations with a top-down approach? It is easier said than done in many cases.

Personal accountability starts with understanding yourself. It is also about creating a personal vision for your life and ensuring that you take all the steps necessary to make that vision a reality. Making a New Year's resolution is a common practice among millions of people at the start of every year. Many people succeed and many fail. In fact, according to Business Insider, 80 percent of New Year's resolutions have been broken by February. Forbes reports that only 8 percent people succeed with their New Year's resolution. What could be the reason? Perhaps it comes down to personal accountability. Holding yourself accountable also has a lot to do with discipline. In fact, the two are complementary. If you lack self-discipline, you may not be able to hold yourself accountable, and if you do hold yourself accountable, you probably have a lot of self-discipline. For this reason, cultivating discipline is crucial in the armed forces. It is a core building block for success.

Use the second axiom to focus on creating accountability within your organization. Use it as a reason to create discipline and alignment, where everyone is focused on generating results in unison and synchronicity. Build a practice (which requires discipline) to help your teams and employees engage with the idea of accountability and discipline on a regular basis. In doing so, you will go a long way to fortifying your organization's strengths and achieving success.

AXIOM 3

PEOPLE WITH MORE KNOWLEDGE ALWAYS LEAD THOSE WITH LESS

Knowledge is power. This is an age-old axiom that has been tried and tested over ages. Education comes in all shapes and sizes; there is more to it that the academic education at school and university. Knowledge, of course, can come from experience, which is derived by working within a business or industry for many years. Knowledge can also be gained as a result of people taking the initiative to learn more, by engaging with customers and so on. The more time you spend on something, the more you learn—the more knowledgeable you become.

Within an organization, success is directly proportional to how knowledgeable employees are. This is a simple and straightforward idea. Because the business world is changing so rapidly, it is essential that everyone in an organization is learning, in order to carry out their roles well. Let us evaluate some key questions that this brings up:

- How does your organization look at knowledge capture and transfer?

- What mechanisms do you have in place to enable the growth of knowledge?

- What programs do you run or offer that push your teams to gain knowledge?

- Is your organization a knowledge desert or a knowledge oasis?

- Do you ask your employees what would help them to increase their knowledge?

- Do you have a budget for helping employees gain and expand knowledge?

- Are you open to creating value for employees, to help them acquire more knowledge so that they can create more value for you?

With a continuously changing education landscape, the majority of which is the result of technological changes, education and training is now available in many forms and flavors. In many cases education pays for itself, because of the value it brings to your organization. Creating an education- and learning-focused culture is a way to value your people; it dramatically improves the quality of your conversations and, as a result, the bottom line for your company.

In addition to training for the technical skills that are very specific to certain professions, there is also an opportunity to learn through Massive Open Online Courses (MOOCs). The world's best universities collaboratively offer courses and programs in an open learning format on topics that appeal to a wide variety of learners. Organizations that utilize this opportunity can help employees gain skills at a very low cost, while aligning learning with a common goal in order to create value within the organization.

Ask yourself:

- How many of your employees are enrolled in MOOCs?

- Have you supported MOOCs for your teams before?

- Does learning form a part of your organizational values?

Imagine that you gather your employees and say this:

"Every employee is expected to increase their knowledge by seeking more knowledge. We are going to work with some key providers of professional development courses that will enhance your skills and capabilities. These courses will not be limited to those directly related to the workplace, but will also relate to hobbies and new skills you are interested in. You'll become more knowledgeable through a process of learning, you'll get new credentials, and you'll improve your overall education and marketability.

"Your progress will be tracked, and you'll compete with your colleagues for your achievements. As a result, you may be eligible to take on longer courses and travel to other countries for specialized educational opportunities, where you'll work with underprivileged adults and kids, imparting knowledge to communities that need assistance. At the end of the year, you will be rewarded for your achievements and efforts, which will have contributed to your life and to those of others you've helped."

You can use the third axiom to change how your organization works from the inside out. You can create resonance, strength, and resiliency from within by empowering your people to embrace new knowledge and, as a result, be more accountable for the outcomes that they and you collectively desire. Far too many organizations focus on generating revenue without recognizing the need for knowledge gain; which is like competing in Formula One without making sure that every nut and bolt in your car is 100 percent tuned.

Check out individual certification options that are specific to your business, and also open learning platforms like Coursera, edX, and the Open University.

HOLD YOURSELF RESPONSIBLE FOR MASTERING YOUR ART

Every goal achievable by an organization depends on the people who work towards the goal. Whatever the department—sales, marketing, operations, human resources, or any other—goals are achieved by people. The problem with people is that they need to be motivated, incentivized, trained, and worked with in order to get the best results.

Let's not forget that organizations create value for people as well. Whether the industry is electronics, consumer goods, travel, shopping, healthcare, or manufacturing, everything is ultimately geared towards how a person will use it and benefit.

The idea of the global family, the idea of family as the most important thing in people's lives, and the idea of treating co-workers or employees are based on the values of the traditional family. In addition to trust, which is important, there is also an element of reliability, and faith that someone will look after you when you are in less than ideal circumstances. Family means being surrounded by people who care for you and want the best for you.

In the business world, it is sometimes hard to build the culture of family. Today's workplaces are chaotic and busy; everyone wants to work fast and punch in and out. Companies small and big face the challenges of employee disengagement and attrition, because the organization is always in a cycle of change. In many cases, employees and leaders do not want to foster a culture of family, because they feel work then becomes too personal when it should be kept separate from family life.

There are many ideas and thoughts that can be exchanged and discussed, and leadership circles take great pleasure in discussing the idea of family, because it definitely is an interesting topic.

To leverage the concept of the family as a pivotal aspect in our lives and to use it as a strength to build upon, you need to strive for self-excellence. This does not mean becoming perfect, because there is no such thing. You need to create the discipline and accountability we talked about earlier, and take the best possible path to achieving personal success. Along this path you will find many challenges, and the goal should be to continuously improve your skills and knowledge, to capture every ounce of value you can in order to achieve success.

Within organizations, this translates to a methodology whereby employees and employee follow a very specific path of alignment, and where results are expected not because you deserve them but because you have formed the idea oath where achieving that specific result is a natural byproduct on the journey of value creation.

When you look around, you see other people who are doing what they need to do. You may see professionals of every type—doctors, scientists, researchers, and so on. You also see people who are not so successful. Some are happy with where they are, as they have accepted their fate. Others are disappointed with where they are and want to go further, but don't see how. Then there are those who work relentlessly to achieve more and to excel by constantly honing their skills. These are the people who really succeed.

Success comes as a result of working on yourself, improving yourself, and staying hungry. It comes by constantly striving to succeed and to be different. Think about successful people you know. They all have one thing in common: They work really hard at becoming an expert and acquiring more skills. True transformation starts with you!

At an individual level, focusing on your core self, embarking on a path of self-improvement, and gaining new skills and expertise put you in the most favorable position to achieve your goals. As an organization, you need a solid core of people who are focused on a central idea of achieving excellence; otherwise, you will face many uphill battles.

The global economy is not dictated just by how fast goods and services are produced, or how fast they can be transported. It is dictated by the speed of response *and* the ingenuity of the ideas behind the goods and services. In today's era of digital disruption, agility and excellence are two faces of the same coin. You absolutely must master the game you are playing and also be fast enough to respond to the demands of the market.

In addition, you must surround yourself with people who have already achieved what you are looking to achieve. It is about really connecting with people and organizations that you admire and that can help you with your goals. Imagine this as a ripple effect, whereby you increase your circle of influence in concentric circles. Because the world is shrinking at a fast pace, due to the development of technology, this ripple effect is happening at many levels. Your circle of influence may expand as you connect with mentors, and then at another level it may expand to accommodate more peers, and so on. Remember, this idea of starting with yourself and then expanding to connect with your immediate family, your work family, and then broader society can only happen if the journey starts from within.

For organizations, the challenge is to engage with people in their own organization and others that can help them realize their vision and become part of their circle of influence. Let us look at some questions:

- As an individual, how many groups are you a part of that directly affect your skills and expertise?

- What efforts have you made to engage in a group activity of excellence in one or more areas?

- As an organization, do you always look at others as customers?

- Who are your closest allies and advisors, those who form your extended family?

For leaders today, this idea translates into reaching out to other leaders and learning from their strengths, ideas, and maybe mistakes. It also means teams and team leaders should think about the larger picture of creating and being part of an ecosystem, rather than having a self-centered existence.

Imagine that you tell staff:

"We need to enhance our sense of community and be able to help others. This starts with being the best version of us, and helping our family, our colleagues, our partners, our customers, and their stakeholders. We do this as an entire organization, and each person plays a key part. Each of us is part of an initiative that helps create more engagement with all of these parties. These are ideas that will help solve big problems and create solutions. Every employee will be able to dedicate 5 percent of their time to developing something in this direction and being part of a larger change."

Use the fourth axiom to create positive change, starting with yourself and then moving out in concentric circles.

AXIOM 5

CREATE OR BE PART OF AN ECOSYSTEM

We work in a global workplace. Technology has given us the ability to work across countries, regions, and continents. The world also has become a smaller place to live in. We travel faster, communicate faster, *live* faster than even five or ten years ago. In fact, experts agree that the rate of change in society is faster than ever, and the reason for this is the technology revolution.

As we head into this era of faster consumption, of specialization, of niche business success, and so much more that is created by technology, we need to understand that the outcomes we need are now dictated by a different way of working.

Here is a way to look at it. Today's world is fast and competitive. Businesses need to be able to specialize in what they do. As a result, being efficient and lean with your business is a must. Organizations need to be able to specialize in core functions and continue to serve customers without disrupting the market more than their business can handle. Today, successful companies such as Walmart, Siemens, and GE are able to not just survive but to thrive, because they work in ecosystems, not isolated silos.

The idea of collaboration has taken on new meaning, and many successful companies are successful because they are able to work within an ecosystem that they not only utilize but also grow, in order to sustain the broader interests of the business. Companies such as Whole Foods, Samsung, and Honda put a tremendous amount of focus on building and supporting the suppliers and businesses that help them to be who they are. In the case of Whole Foods, they actively support local farmers, suppliers, and other stakeholders that are connected to the chain of value creation within which they operate. The same goes for every organization that delivers products and services successfully in today's competitive world.

Let's us look at some key questions that may help us dig deeper:

- Does your business support a larger ecosystem of partners?

- Are you involved in any industry initiatives?

- Do you bring external influence to your organization through dialogue and new connections?

- Have you contributed to some initiative purely to support industry and the value created?

- Are you personally part of some broader initiative that does not support your direct growth?

If your answer to any of these questions is no, then give it some thought and discuss it with your peers and colleagues.

The environment we live in determines how we live. We have a responsibility not only to keep our immediate environment in a good condition but also to support the broader community, the world, in making the world a better place.

What if you told your employees the following?

"As an organization, we will take part in drives to create a cleaner environment, through plant-a-tree, recycling, and other activities we can do right away. Our goal is to plant at least one million new trees across all our office locations worldwide. We will adopt communities that need help with challenges they have with the environment, such as providing clean drinking water. We will also support vertical farming communities, offering our facilities as a place for startup companies to begin work. And we will encourage every employee to be part of a personal environment development program, for which they will receive a commendation and be in the running for a community contribution award, overseen by our new Sustainable Living Community Team."

Use the fifth axiom to seek opportunities to grow as an organization and as an individual—to grow the ecosystem around you. Just like a forest is necessary to support life, so we need an ecosystem to support a business. In fact, having competition is a great thing, because it validates the need for a product and can provide you with innumerable opportunities to differentiate yourself as a leader. Take the initiative to analyze what opportunities are available to which you can contribute without any immediate financial gain.

HELP CREATE VALUE FOR OTHERS

When a group of people—an organization—decide to create positive change by creating value through, say, a product or a service, what is the one pivotal thing they do? Any guesses? Let's reframe the question. If money were not an object and you did not have to work to make money, what would you be doing and why? If you have not guessed already, the answers lie in understanding what we do for others.

Behind anything and everything, people are involved. Whether organizations make toys or trucks, cars or catamarans, everything gets used by people. Successful organizations take this idea and embody it in their corporate DNA.

Here are a few company mission statements:

- Life is Good: "To spread the power of optimism."

- sweetgreen: "To inspire healthier communities by connecting people to real food."

- Patagonia: "Build the best product, cause no unnecessary harm, use business to inspire and implement solutions to the environmental crisis."

- American Express: "We work hard every day to make American Express the world's most respected service brand."

- Honest Tea: "... to create and promote great-tasting, healthy, organic beverages."

- IKEA: "To create a better everyday life for the many people."

The central point in all of these mission statements is not being the richest company in the world or driving revenues through the roof, it is offering value to others. Money and revenue are side effects of that value created.

I once met a man who kept on hammering the fact that his company was a *sales* company. It never made sense to me how he expected results (which he never got). Unless managers, leaders, owners, and CEOs believe in helping others and transmit that to their teams and all the people who work for the organization, success is going to be a tough cookie.

I am sure you have heard of the elevator pitch. What does your elevator pitch say about your organization? Does it focus on helping people and creating value? Here is an example. If you are a salesperson, does your elevator pitch focus on your product or service? Would you say:

- "Hi, I'm John and I work for a software company. We sell cloud-based accounting systems."

- "Hi, I'm Susan. I work for a drug company."

- "Hi, my name is Bob and I'm an accountant."

All of these elevator pitch intros miss a key part. They do not express the real reason you are in business and the truth about who you are.

What you do and your business are two different things. You could be a salesperson, but your business is not software sales; it is helping businesses manage their finances. You could be working for a drug company, but you're not passionate about your role and so are unable to say you work for a company that plays a pivotal role in healthcare and helping people deal with sickness.

For the final elevator pitch, what a difference it would make to say, "Hi, my name is Bob and I help people efficiently manage their finances, so that they can save for retirement, enjoy their life, and not have any debt." Isn't that the true calling of an accountant?

Passion transfers, and passion brings about positive results, be it in the shape of sales, more business, or good relationships.

Going back to helping others, successful businesses are built on creating value, helping others, and facilitating positive outcomes for others. Of course, you need good management and great people to succeed as well, but management and people need a value-based workplace where they can thrive.

This is how your organization can look:

"Helping others with their goals and dreams is key to being able to achieve your goals and dreams. We are going to make sure that we help others in any way we can, through support, education, facilitation, and knowledge. All of us together are a vast bank of knowledge, and there are people in the world who can benefit from this knowledge and have better lives, providing for their families and being helpful to others. The key point is being able to support others in achieving their goals, and as a result being a small reason for someone else's success. We will create a program to help facilitate this, by joining up with some key development organizations that provide this type of support to others. We may bring people into the workplace to work with them on a one-to-one basis or as a group, where we as a team or as individuals help with their problems."

Take a look at companies that are very successful where you are. Find out how they help people, how they get a positive outcome, and how they monetize this idea. Once you have found the formula for helping others get what they want, you will automatically reach your destiny and achieve your goals. Guaranteed.

AXIOM 7

THE GREATEST CURRENCY IS GRATITUDE

If you follow a religion, you are likely taught to express gratitude. But you do not need to be religious to have gratitude. Irrespective of your faith, gratitude is a key factor for enabling a mindset of success, first for yourself and then for your teams and the people you work with.

Today, organizations are challenged by the mix of generations within the workforce. When a wide range of people of different ages work together, many get along but some do not. We often hear about Millennials and how they are creating havoc in the workplace, because the older methods do not suit them, but organizations do not want to let go of their old habits. This clash between generations will never go away. Period. No matter what age you live in, there will always be different generations and they will always have different needs. Meanwhile, many companies are spending millions of dollars on figuring out how to deal with this generation gap.

In this era of technological disruption and fading attention spans, there is another issue: employees not giving their best every day. How can leaders ensure employees are happy and contribute to the organization, not just with their time but also with their skills and ideas?

Here are questions to gauge the overall picture of your organization and how it functions:

- Does your organization focus on helping employees bring the best of their talent?

- Do you have initiatives that encourage non-work-related activities?

- How many of your HR programs are focused on internal engagement?

Now let's go deeper, and discuss gratitude within the organization and at home, for both organizational as well as personal development.

From Australia's Aboriginals to the Arabs, the Babylonians to the Berbers of Morocco, everyone knows about gratitude, and in every culture it is viewed as a good thing that ultimately benefits the person who practices it.

If you are an avid book reader or movie watcher, you probably know of *The Secret*. It is a book and TV show that showcased New Age experts and their take on things in our modern world, including how to achieve your goals and practice gratitude. A really nice read or a watch.

How do you take the idea of gratitude and translate it into the workplace? How can it be applied so that it does not hurt productivity, but increases the overall morale of employees and helps create a profitable and efficient business environment? The answer may lie in a practice connected to gratitude, yet different: acknowledgement.

We live in the era of the rewards economy. Consumer engagement is the biggest need of a business that seeks growth. Experts suggest that in the future the biggest and most expensive commodity will be human attention, and they could be right. How do you then engage with your customers, your employees, peers, and others in this age of distractions? The answer lies in creating and enabling a *rewards and acknowledgement practice*.

Let me ask:

- Does your organization have a rewards and acknowledgement practice in place?

- Is this a core area of focus for your organization or not as much as it should be?

- Does your organization seek attention from stakeholders, and is marketing your biggest resource right now?

If you answered yes to any of these questions then you need to rethink your engagement strategy. Enabling a rewards and acknowledgment practice across the board and at various levels will significantly open up your possibilities.

Here is how to activate the seventh axiom of gratitude:

- Create an employee rewards program. The reward does not necessarily have to be a financial incentive; movie tickets, a pat on the back, and many other simple things work as well.

- Make acknowledgement part of your business practice and utilize it every day.

- Reward your customers and your partners when the time is right.

- Express your thanks to customers on every possible occasion. After all, they are the reason you are in business.

- Help create goodwill between your business and your stakeholders by positively reinforcing the value they bring to you.

- Ask your team to take an active role in enabling the rewards system across the board.

When it comes to gratitude, we can all do a bit more. Practicing gratitude will really enhance the quality of our lives and make us sees beyond the problems we face on an everyday basis, even while we are poised to solve problems and to weather any storms. It will also help change the state of our physical and mental health, and create an atmosphere of calm and giving in the workplace and at home. Practicing gratitude means not complaining, but making an effort to look on the positive side of life while trying to find a solution for the negatives we encounter.

This last axiom will change us more than any other, and it is the greatest value creator for all of us.

21

THE JOURNEY JUST ENDED...
OR DID IT?

Over the next two years, Max and his team of empowered contributors ended up creating one of the world's most envied companies. Collectively, they created more social change than they could have imagined, not only affecting their local communities but also underprivileged communities around the world.

To this day, the seven axioms still remain at the heart of Max's organization, which he has expanded into philanthropy, education, and healthcare. His employees are no longer bound to produce results, but are responsible for creating great change.

Today, Max and Aira are in Cambodia, where one of their subsidiaries is helping small business owners learn about the internet and how it can change their lives. Next week, they will both be in

Shanghai, where the world's largest e-commerce company wants to know how to use the seven axioms to change how the organization functions and to help change the world around.

Have you started thinking about how the seven axioms can change everything you do and know…?

And the story continues…

7 AXIOMS OF VALUE CREATION

ENGAGE

The definition of connecting with others has changed. Technology has a lot to do with it. Seek out the different ways in your customers, partners and associates now value communication channels and change the way you engage with others.

LEARN

A Pivotal step in being successful in todays era of change. Learning should never stop and you should embark on a continuous learning path.

COLLABORATE

Today you cannot create success on your own. It is impossible to be bale to manage the complexity of a business environment and succeed. Create partnerships with other companies and individuals that can help you unlock more value than you can do alone.

PEOPLE

Organizations that do not focus on ensuring people at every level are served to the best of their abilities will fall into an abyss of unproductivity and recession. Focus on people.

ACCOUNTABILITY

Organizations that are future focused and success oriented do not just expect accountability within their four walls, but embed it into every person they interface with.

VALUE

We need to shift our thinking from being only financially driven to being value creators. Organizations and individuals who consistently think about value creation as a goal outperform those that favor only revenue generation, financial abundance and short sighted goals.

ACTUALIZE

Beyond any goal and need is the ability to reach the state of actualization. This is above all of your basic needs are met and you understand the value of reaching a higher stage in your organizations life or even yours.

DING
OF
OGY

GING THE WORLD
CEEDING

IAN KHAN'S
MASTERMIND
GROUP

"AS A FUTURIST MY ONLY GOAL IS TO HELP YOU GET WHERE YOU WANT WITH TOMORROW IN MIND" - IAN

- A GUIDED SUCCESS ROADMAP
- BI WEEKLY CALLS WITH YOUR PEER GROUP
- YEARLY FACE TO FACE EVENTS

VISIT WWW.IANKHAN.COM

THE INNOV
MASTERCL

- THE BUSINESS SUCCES SECRETS
- UNCOVER YOUR TRUE INNOVATOR
- BUSINESS SUCCESS BLUEPRINT

VISIT WWW.IANKHAN.COM